EUL VERLAG

Prof. Wolfgang Chr. Fischer

Private Households and Money Supply

With a Foreword by
Prof. Kenneth K. Mwenda, PhD, LLD,
Washington DC, USA

EUL VERLAG

Bibliografische Information der Deutschen Nationalbibliothek

Die Deutsche Nationalbibliothek verzeichnet diese Publikation in der Deutschen Nationalbibliografie; detaillierte bibliografische Daten sind im Internet über <http://dnb.d-nb.de> abrufbar.

ISBN 978-3-8441-0265-9
1. Auflage August 2013

JOSEF EUL VERLAG GmbH
Brandsberg 6
53797 Lohmar
Tel.: 0 22 05 / 90 10 6-6
Fax: 0 22 05 / 90 10 6-88
E-Mail: info@eul-verlag.de
http://www.eul-verlag.de

Bei der Herstellung unserer Bücher möchten wir die Umwelt schonen. Dieses Buch ist daher auf säurefreiem, 100% chlorfrei gebleichtem, alterungsbeständigem Papier nach DIN 6738 gedruckt.

The roasting spit in this European medieval kitchen was driven automatically by a propeller—the black cloverleaf-like structure in the upper left.[1]

JAMES COOK UNIVERSITY
AUSTRALIA

Research Monograph
School of Law, Faculty of Law, Business & Creative Arts,
James Cook University, Townsville, North Queensland, Australia

[1] http://en.wikipedia.org/wiki/Kitchen

This Research Monograph
is dedicated to my Academic Lecturer and Supervisor,
who inspired me in economic matters concerning private households.

Fritz W. Meyer
(8.11.1907 – 4.3.1980)
Dr.rer.pol.habil.
Professor of Economics
Direktor des Institut für Wirtschaftspolitik
Rechts- und Staatswissenschaftliche Fakultät
Rheinische Friedrich-Wilhelms-Universität
Bonn, Germany

Professor Dr. Meyer second person[2] on the left as one of the five member of the first Council of Economic Experts, appointed by the Federal President of the Federal Republic of Germany, in the Federal President's Office 1964[3]

---

2 Bundesarchiv_B_145_Bild-F017490-0004,_Bonn,_Die_"Fünf_Weisen"_beim_Bundespräsidenten .jpg. In http://de.wikipedia.org/wiki/Fritz_W._Meyer

3 The *Council of Economic Experts* is an academic body advising German policy makers on questions of economic policy since 1963 for the period of five years. It was set up by law in 1963 with the objective to assess the macroeconomic development of Germany. It also aims to aid the public and economically relevant institutions in making informed judgments about economic developments. It enjoys complete independence with respect to its advisory activities. The Council's reports and assessments have since become an essential part of German economic policy making and have notably influenced political decisions.

Jessie Mary Grey Street (née Lillingston) (1889-1970)
Jessie Street at the United Women's Conference in San Francisco, 19 May 1945[4]

> "I realised how wrong it was that money, the economic blood-stream of the whole community, should be controlled by individuals for their own benefit and profit."[5]

[4] http://en.wikipedia.org/wiki/Jessie_Street
[5] Coltheart, Lenore (Editor) (2004) Jessie Street, A revised autobiography, The Federation Press, Sydney, p. 81

Soup Kitchen Montreal 1931[6]

[6] http://en.wikipedia.org/wiki/Soup_kitchen

Foreword

-------\-------

Sounding an alarm to private households against over-dependency on money supply from the national economy, this book, *Private Households and Money Supply*, contends that such over-dependency often deprives many private households of other sources of income such as their own initiative at providing to the market private goods and services that can earn them a better income for improving their living standards.

The author, Professor Dr. Wolfgang Chr. Fischer, provides an excellent treatment of household incomes in Western societies. He makes a compelling case of how household incomes can be improved and how they can contribute to uplifting the standard of living of many citizens. And the central thesis of the book highlighted above is in tandem with such other inspiring works as Aldous Huxley's *Brave New World*, David Caplovitz's *The Poor Pay More*, and Sir Martin Rees's *Our Final Century*.

Notably, Professor Fischer's *Private Households and Money Supply* is on the different side of the chasm from the all too often euphoric sentiments about Western civilization. In this vein, *Private Households and Money Supply* brings forward arguments that are in stark contrast to works such as Niall Ferguson's *Civilization – The West and the Rest.* Contrastingly, Professor Fischer's *Private Households and Money Supply* posits that there are many signs that point to the imminent downfall of Western societies today as well as to the final end of colonization by European powers.

In setting out the context of the study, Chapter 1 of *Private Households and Money Supply* examines micro- and macro-economic fundamentals of private household production. The said chapter addresses salient aspects of the history of economic thought and private household production. It also examines some definitions of the terms 'private household' and 'private household production'. Thereafter, the chapter proceeds to look at pertinent aspects of implementing private household production. Then, the nexus between private household production and economic division of labour is fleshed out.

Chapter 2 focuses on private household production and the 'free market' philosophy. It delves into the intricate relationship between consumer sovereignty and a free market economy. Also, an analysis of private household compositions is carried out, including an analysis of equipment owned by those households that have household appliances. The said chapter then proceeds to examine the concept of market power of some service and retail providers. Closely related to that is the role that consumer associations play as well as some prospects for government intervention in private household production.

Chapter 3 turns the debate to examine the position of private households in a cash economy. Complementing that discussion, Chapter 4 examines how economic inflation affects private households. While the history of economic thought about inflation is considered in Chapter 4, together with an analysis of the inflationary process, Chapter 3 precedes that discussion with an analysis of private households in a cash economy, focusing on Goods and Services Taxes (GST), on the one hand, and the concepts of Tax Evasion and Tax Avoidance, on the other.

Chapter 5 concludes the study by examining the concept of self-sufficient private household production versus money dependency. The main principles of self-sufficient private household production are examined, and the chapter sheds some light on the economic future of many Western societies.

No doubt, this is a timely, well-argued and concisely written book that adds great value to the ever growing body of literature on private household incomes. Professor Fischer writes with such great clarity that even the non-economist reader will find this book a valuable read. Indeed, this is a book that will be useful to many a scholar and reader from different disciplinary backgrounds as well as to different geographical regions. Professor Fischer should be commended for bringing out this excellent study. It not only provides a fresh perspective to the debate on household incomes, but it also provides food for thought on the sustainability of certain fundamental assumptions underpinning the ideology of a free-market economy.

Professor Kenneth K. Mwenda, PhD, LLD[7]
Washington DC, USA

---

[7] A Rhodes Scholar, Prof. Kenneth K. Mwenda is Program Manager, Voice Secondment Program of the World Bank, Washington DC. He also serves as Extraordinary Professor of Law at the University of Pretoria, South Africa, as well as Adjunct Professor of Law at American University Washington College of Law in Washington DC.

Preface

-------ꟙ------

This Research Project about *"Private Households and Money Supply"* aims to contribute to the knowledge and understanding of the significance of private household production and often this crucial issue had been regarded in the relevant literature of Economics as a quantité négligeable.

Furthermore I offer my genuine thanks to *Professor Dr. Stephen Graw,* Head of School of Law, James Cook University, Townsville, Australia, who generously supported my research work. Furthermore I offer my thanks to *Mrs Shirley Jones,* School Manager, *Mrs Bronwyn Murray,* School Secretary and to the Administrative Officer *Mrs Marianne Dunkerley* who gave kindly of their time and expertise in administrative support.

Additionally I would like to express my sincere thanks to the retired Solicitor *Mr Richard Anthony Lindsay,* Townsville, the Stockbroker *Mr Daniel Goulding* BEc, Townsville, the retired Executive Director of the Australian Companies Institute *Mr Michael M Gallagher* CA (Scotland), Sydney, and to the Neurologist & Psychiatrist Dr.med. *Erich Krausbeck,* Bad Ems, Germany, for their valuable input.

I am very grateful to *Ms Karen Kuhlmann,* Editorial Office, Eul Verlag, Köln, Germany, for her various assistance in preparing the manuscript for its final publication.

Finally, I owe a great debt of gratitude to my wife *Mrs Janelle Margaret Fischer,* who revised the manuscript, composed the Index, and carefully prepared it for publication.

Wolfgang Christian Fischer
Magnetic Island, Australia, South Pacific, July 2013

CONTENTS

ABBREVIATIONS

ABS	Australian Bureau of Statistics
A$	Australian Dollar
€	Euro
DM	Deutsche Mark
EVS	Einkommens- und Verbrauchsstichprobe 2008 (Income and Consumption Sample Survey)
EU	European Union
GDP	Gross Domestic Product
GST	Goods & Services Tax
IMF	International Monetary Fund
KPD	Communist Party of Germany
US	United States of America
US$	American Dollar
VAT	Value Added Tax
WWI	World War I (1914-1918)
WWII	World War II (1939-1945)

Introduction

-------ꕥ------

This research is focussed on the development of private household production and its various factors which could help to minimize the loss of a buffer function for times of economic downturn. Once the ability to establish a self-sufficient household with most of its vital areas of production is lost, the dependency on the market is inevitably created. Income in terms of money has to be the source of the members of the household's activities to maintain a reasonable living. Subsequently the dependency on the state of affairs of the national economy and given the integration into the global market the dependency on international markets becomes vital.

Centuries ago the political economics was devoted to the development of private household production. Especially in the 19th century *Karl Bücher* and *Gustav Schmoller* tried to work out a historical integration of the private household production into the economic division of labour as a development from the self-sufficient private household up to the modern economy with division of labour.[8] In particular at the beginning of the industrialization, and under the impression of that time and taking into account future possible social and economic transformations, there was established an unchallenged and widely held thesis that in the course of the industrial and social progress the private household production will be inevitably diminished, with some exemptions related to economic crises. Areas of the private household production with a much greater economic efficiency will be possibly integrated into the external private business and public sector.[9]

This prognosis of development advocated by *Friedrich Engels* and *August Bebel*, among others, has the basic idea that the private household is an obsolete traditional institution and the enclosed private household production is abolished, leading to a classical consumption unit. Furthermore the advocates for such a radical change of the private household production have argued that the private household

---

[8] Fischer, Wolfgang Chr. (1982) Entwicklung der privaten Hauswirtschaft, Baltmannsweiler, Germany, p. 1

[9] ibid.

production created a substantial disadvantage for the development of emancipation of women, and they strongly demanded that women be integrated into the external sector.[10]

This research demonstrates that ultimately the development of the private household production, including the areas for instance of nutrition, storage, shopping, cleaning, clothes, natural domestic production and personal care of household members, is not primarily depending on the level of the economic division of labour, but substantially depending on the realised social and economic order and their further development. In his doctoral dissertation *Wolfgang Fischer* had proven in detail that the development of private household production is primarily depending on the existing and pursued social and economic order, rather than on the level of the present and future development of the economic division of labour as well as on an integrated long term process which follows in historical phases.[11]

In *Western Societies,* with their capitalist economic order, the private households have undergone substantial changes: The possibilities for private household production declined in various areas, for instance the raising up of children, caring for elderly people, food production and meal preparation, production of household durables, clothes etcetera. Further and further dependency of households on income and money supply to acquire articles or items for consumption arises. The development of smaller and smaller household composition leads to both adults/parents in the so-called atomistic household (two parents plus two children at the most), including the development of one person households (nearly 50% of all households), having to work and to shifting of a lot of household functions which are outside their own ability to fulfil – when a cleaning lady is employed the Gross Domestic Product grows, if she is then not employed anymore the GDP goes down, in other words household chores and household work is not valued in economic accounting.

There exists the household dependency on the national economy and what is provided, but today the dependency is imposed even on the international market, in particular for Australia on the production of Chinese consumption goods and on many other Asian economies, e.g. from Vietnam the fish supply.

---

[10] Fischer, Wolfgang Chr. (1982) Entwicklung der privaten Hauswirtschaft, Baltmannsweiler, Germany, p. 1

[11] Fischer, Wolfgang (1972) Sozial-Ökonomische Aspekte der Entwicklung der Privaten Hauswirtschaft, Inaugural-Dissertation, Rechts- und Staatswissenschaftliche Fakultät der Rheinischen Friedrich-Wilhelms-Universität zu Bonn, Universitäts Druckerei Bonn

It is to prove that the author's predictions from 1971 in his doctoral dissertation at the University of Bonn, Germany, have mostly come true and that the situation of an empty household with very little household production has been successfully achieved by the marketing and marketing research of larger and smaller companies which followed the way of a capitalistic system and where for the business the profits are possible?.

The amazing lack of knowledge for household production and the disappearance of the teaching and research of home economics or domestic science, plus other factors such as women's liberation, capitalist lifestyle, non value of household work, have all contributed to changes in the retail structure in an economy including concentration of the retail industry. There is neglecting of minority demand - if someone wants to repair his shoes, clothing, or even wants to produce some clothes from scratch - this becomes very difficult because those retail outlets are very rare and hard to access whereas in former times this was a major interest of department stores.

It is worth to mention that even in former times in the so called 'rich' circles in England the conversation did not include so much the subject 'money'. In a recent publication *Deborah Devonshire,* who was born as Deborah *Mitford* in 1920 and was the youngest child of *Lord Redesdale*[12], revealed:

> "...We all knew that if Muv had been in charge of our family finances everything might have been different. As it was, she had to juggle with what she was given and somehow remain solvent; intuition took her in the right direction and she never overspent. She was the one who put down roots and became part of the place where she lived, and it was she who bore the brunt of my father's extravagances and unlucky investments. It must have been hard for her each time we moved but I never heard her say so. I wonder now how much farve told her when another crisis was building up. As children, none of us was privy to such discussions – if indeed they took place. Money was not spoken about as it is now, when it

---

12 David Bertram Ogilvy Freeman-Mitford, 2nd Baron Redesdale, (13 March 1878 – 17 March 1958), was an English landowner and was the father of the Mitford sisters, in whose various novels and memoirs he is depicted. David Bertram Ogilvy Freeman-Mitford, 2nd Baron Redesdale, from Wikipedia, at http://en.wikipedia.org/wiki/David_Freeman-Mitford,_2nd_Baron_Redesdale, viewed 19 Jul 2012.

> is often the sole subject of conversation, with a bit of illness thrown in..."[13]

Finally, one has to bear in mind that technically the majority of the presented figures are not up to date, however the figures still have their validity in the sense of illustrating trends which are at the present time nonetheless remarkably applicable.[14]

---

13 Devonshire, Deborah (2010) Wait For Me! Memoirs of the Youngest Mitford Sister, John Murray, London, Great Britain.

14 The author had minor research funds available and therefore had to limit the variety of figures to those easily and freely accessible ones.

Chapter 1

-------ഇ------

Micro and Macro Economic Fundamentals of Private Household Production

1.1 History of Economic Thought and Private Household Production

Early in the history of economic thought the economics of the antique already deals with the private household and in particular with the private household production, the main subject which is represented by *Xenophon* and *Aristotle*.[15]

Aristotle differentiates between *'Ökonomik'* and *'Chrematistik'*, whereas he names 'Ökonomik' as a science of private household and 'Chrematistik' as a science of business. The term 'Ökonomik' originates very closely to the private household and leads to the economic and social administration of a house and 'Öikonomiké' therefore is the science of how to run a household in a good sense.[16] The 'Ökonomik' deals therefore as a science with the total human relationships and all the activities in a house including the relationship between men and women, parents and children, landlord and slaves, and the goals to achieve the tasks which are set up to run a household and the agricultural production.[17] Contrary to the 'Ökonomik' is the 'Chrematistik' which is a commerce-orientated science and predominantly deals with the business of merchandise and money exchange. According to Aristotle there

---

[15] Brunner, Otto (1952) Die alteuropäsche "Ökonomik", in: Zeitschrift für Nationalökonomie, Bd. 13, Wien, S. 114-139, p. 115
Egner, Erich (1953) Die Rolle des Haushalts in der Geistesgeschichte, in: Hauswirtschaft und Wissenschaft, Jg. 1, Heft 1, Hamburg, pp. 9-18
Schweitzer, Rosmarie von (1977) From the economic writings of Aristotle to Home Economics in the German Federal Republic today. In: Journal of Consumer Studies and Home Economics 1, pp. 41-50
Tschammer-Osten, Berndt (1973) Der private Haushalt in einzelwirtschaftlicher Sicht. Prolegomena zur einzelwirtschaftlichen Dogmengeschichte und Metholodolgie, Berlin, pp. 17-24

[16] Egner, Erich (1964) Die volkswirtschaftliche Funktion der Familienhaushalte, in: Jahrbuch für Sozialwissenschaft, Bd. 15, Göttingen, p. 205

[17] Brunner, Otto (1952) Die alteuropäsche "Ökonomik", p. 116

is a moral difference between those two contrary sciences in the sense that the private household and its production and organizing it is regarded as natural and well accepted whereas the money exchange and the merchandise accumulation is a self-orientated goal, which is completely against human nature. Transformed into the current economic thought 'Chrematistik' would be thinking from the market in which private households have very little room left. *Brunner* and *Egner* regarded as the source of the modern economics in the 'Chrematistik' and not in the 'Ökonomik'.[18]

In the antique economic thought the self-sufficient private household production is a central subject which was called by *Rodbertus* as *'Oikos'*. *Bücher* names this *'Oikos'* as a closed private household production and he regards it in his theory of sequences of historical stages as the first one, then the second stage would be the city economy, then the third one is the national economy.[19]

The term *'Oikos'* contains not only a large society within a house in the sense of relatives and servants but is according to *Max Weber* also an authoritarian administratively large household of a prince, of a large landholder and a wealthy merchant, in which all of them have as their leading motive, not the accumulation of money in a capitalistic way, but the organised natural supply of the needs of a master. [20] Economic thought of the antique and its predominant subject of investigation of the private household and private household production was taken over by the *Roman agricultural science* but with a much stronger emphasis on the private household production including the agricultural estate. The Latin term *'familia'* means in its real sense not only a unity of relatives and servants in the form of a larger family but also a unified society living together under one roof. That means that the term "familia' is all tangible and non-tangible goods and chattels including the male and female farm workers.[21] However one has to bear in mind that the *Oikos* of the Antique and the Roman large manor cannot be defined in the same sense as *Bücher's* closed household production. A complete self-sufficiency of this economic unit, closed household production, was never the dominant goal of this economic unit because temporarily and even with profits involved a delivery of self-produced goods to the market was included in their economic goals and

---

18 Egner, Erich (1967) Zum Verständnis des hauswirtschaftlichen Sturkturwandels, in: Beiträge zur Ökonomie von Haushalt und Verbrauch, Heft 3, Berlin, pp. 15-16

19 Bücher, Karl (1917) Die Entstehung der Volkswirtschaft, Erste Sammlung, 10. Aufl., Tübingen, p. 92

20 Weber, Max (1925) Wirtschaft und Gesellschaft, in: Grundriss der Sozialoekonomik, III. Abteilung, 1. Halbband, zweite, vermehrte Auflage, Tuebingen, p. 212

21 König, René (1946) Materialien zur Soziologie der Familie, Beiträge zur Soziologie und Sozialphilosophie, Bd. 1, Bern, p. 74

achievements. The economic thought with central recognition of private household is then represented in the following scholastic or *Christian economic thought* of the mediaeval ages and furthermore in the *German head of household literature* of the 16th and until the 18th century. This literature is a science of the house in a broader sense and this type of literature contains a conglomerate of ethnic, sociological, pedagogical, medical, and agricultural subjects. It is not only a simple accumulation of isolated knowledge but it is regarded as the principle of order and law of the head of the household.[22] In the centre of this broader house is the *Head of the household (Hausväterliteratur)*, he and only he alone is able to achieve a unity of the household community and therefore of the whole house. One has to bear in mind that the author of this literature of the *Head of household* had not in mind a brutal, dominant, petty bourgeois head of the household, but saw in their head of household an idealistic, wise and well-rounded father of a family with metaphysical background. As remarkable authors of this literature it could be named: *Wolf Helmhard von Hohberg,* 'Georgica curiosa oder Adeliges Land- und Feldleben' (1682), *Johannes Coler,* 'Oeconomia ruralis et domestica' (1593), and *Johann Joachim Becher.*

In the middle of the 19th century *Wilhelm Heinrich von Riehl* is complaining in his populist publication 'Naturgeschichte des Volkes als Grundlage einer deutschen Social-politik' (1851-1869)[23] about the downfall of this type of house.[24] He regards the more and more forthcoming industrial revolution and industrial development as the major factor for the downfall and for the deterioration of longstanding traditions for an economic activity within a house or what he calls the whole house.[25] With a lot of emphasis he tries to convince ordinary people and politicians that the new economic thought and the industrial development are the evil and destroying the household production in the sense of a self-sufficient unit. In particular he regards the solution of the unity of household production and agricultural self-sufficiency as substantially dangerous for the general moral of the people and he is propagating the substitution of the farm production as a predominant social policy.

---

22 Brunner, Otto (1956) Hausvaeterliteratur, in: Handwoerterbuch der Sozialwissenschaften, 5. Band, Goettingen, p. 93

23 http://de.wikipedia.org/wiki/Wilhelm_Heinrich_Riehl

24 Riehl, Wilhelm Heinrich (1965) Die Familie, 3. Auflage, Stuttgart 1861, and: Die Naturgeschichte des Volkes als Grundlage einer deutschen Socialpolitik, Bd. 2: Die bürgerliche Gesellschaft, elfte Auflage, Berlin und Stuttgart 1930, and: Die Arbeiter, Eine Volksrede aus dem Jahre 1848, in: Die Eigentumslosen; Der deutsche Pauperismus und die Emanzipationskrise in Darstellungen und Deutungen der zeitgenössischen Literatur. Hrsg. Carl Jantke und Dietrich Hilger, Freiburg und München

25 ibid., p. 183

With regret *von Riehl* realised this loss of an economic thought orientated on private households as essentially a consequence of the *mercantilism* of the 18th century. The major subject of the mercantilist commerce science as an economic theory of the absolutistic state science is predominantly orientated to analysing commerce and trade. To foster these two areas of economic activity was the first call of mercantilist economic policy which was placed into the centre of the economic activity of the sovereign. With this economic concept follows a theory of economic activity which is primarily based on the rational decisions of people taking part in market activity.

Wilhelm Heinrich von Riehl (1823-1897)[26]

Early in the 19th century the so called *'Utopian'* socialists like *Robert Owen, Charles Fourier* and *Henri de Saint-Simon,* who inspired *Karl Marx and Friedrich Engels*[27], regarded the progressive development of capitalism through the industrialisation within relatively free markets as detrimental to the well-being of ordinary people.[28] The term is most often applied to those socialists who lived in the first quarter of the 19th century who were ascribed the label 'utopian' by later socialists – mostly by

26 http://de.wikipedia.org/wiki/Wilhelm_Heinrich_Riehl

27 http://en.wikipedia.org/wiki/Utopian_socialism

28 Fischer, Wolfgang Chr. (1990) Zentralisierung der Hauswirtschaft - eine Alternative zur traditionellen Aufgabenverteilung im privaten Haushalt? In: Zeitschrift Erwägen Wissen Ethik (EWE) vormals: Ethik und Sozialwissenschaften (EuS) zu Genderthemen, EuS-Heft 2, Jg. 1, pp. 286-288, Paderborn, Germany

Karl Marx and *Friedrich Engels* in their *Communist Manifesto of 1848*[29] – as a negative term, in order to imply naiveté and to dismiss their ideas as fanciful or unrealistic. They were early socialist or quasi-socialist intellectuals who created hypothetical visions of egalitarian, communalist, meritocratic, or other notions of 'perfect' societies without actually concerning themselves with the manner in which these societies could be created or sustained.[30]

One of their solutions to this misery was the establishment of 'closed' societies within a restricted area or even in a compound, where the private household production had been more or less centralised to create a society, which was able to work and live without the shackles of a bourgeois household in a capitalistic system. Some examples were the formation an *Owenite* commune called *New Lanark* – roughly 2,500 people lived at New Lanark, many from the poorhouses of Glasgow and Edinburgh in Scotland – and *New Harmony* in Indiana in the United States, by *Robert Owen,* a Welsh businessman with social intentions to help his employees.[31]

Charles Fourier was another 'utopian' socialist, who rejected the industrial revolution. He invented the concept of *phalanstère*, units of people based on a theory of passions and of their combination. Several colonies based on Fourier's ideas were founded in the United States by *Albert Brisbane* and *Horace Greeley.*[32]

A *phalanstère* was based on the idea of a phalanx; this self-contained community ideally consisted of 1500-1600 people working together for mutual benefit. A few colonies were founded in the United States like *La Reunion (Dallas), Brook Farm* and *North American Phalanx.*[33] Further utopian communities were *Corning, Iowa, Whiteway Colony, Life and Labor Commune, Kaweah Colony, Oneida Community and Ruskin Colony.*[34]

---

29 The Communist Manifesto *(Das Kommunistische Manifest),* originally titled *Manifesto of the Communist Party* (German: *Manifest der Kommunistischen Partei*), is a short 1848 publication written by the political theorists Karl Marx and Friedrich Engels

30 http://en.wikipedia.org/wiki/Utopian_socialism

31 Ordinaire, Eduard: Abriß der von Fourier vorgeschlagenen Einrichtung der lusterweckenden Gewerbsthätigkeit (industrie attrayante), in: Archiv der poltischen Oekonomie und Polizeiwissenschaft, 2. Bd., Heidelberg 1835. This development has been documented precisely by Robert Liefmann, in: Liefmann, Robert (1922) Die Kommunistischen Gemeinden in Nordamerika, Jena

32 http://en.wikipedia.org/wiki/Phalanst%C3%A8re

33 http://en.wikipedia.org/wiki/Phalanst%C3%A8re

34 ibid.

Perspective view of the urban area of *Charles Fourier's Phalanstère*[35]

By the end of the 19th century the classical socialists based in their propagated so called 'scientific socialism' originated by *Karl Marx* and *Friedrich Engels* were convinced that the existence of private households and their private production of goods and services will be made obsolete through the extensive development of capitalism and will end up in centralised private household production. This means that the private household production would become an institutionalised service for the members of a socialistic system. Furthermore the centralisation of private households and their disappearance from the scene of individual management of private affairs would be beneficial for the emancipation of women.[36]

The political claim for a centralisation of the private household production – in its various forms – in the sense of a radical and complete abolishment of the private household production and its transformation into other types of public organised satisfaction of private needs has the underlying thought that with increased industrialisation in the non-private household sectors achieved, increasing productivity in the private household production has only little benefits.[37] *Adolph* for

---

35 ibid.

36 Zetkin, Clara (1926) Lenin ruft die werktätigen Frauen; Artikel Lenins zur Frauenfrage, Berlin, p. 36

37 A precise presentation of the Centralisation of the private household production can be found in:
Strauβ, Beatrice (1927) Die Konsumtionswirtschaft; Ihre Parallelentwicklung mit der Frauenberufsfrage; Diss. Frankfurt
Richter, Claire (1919) Das Ökonomiat; Hauswirtschaftlicher Groβbetrieb als Selbstzweck; Berlin
Essig, Olga (1920) Der hauswirtschaftliche Groβbetrieb; Eine wirtschaftswissenschaftliche Studie; Frankfurt
Adolph, Robert (1919) Einküchenwirtschaft als soziale Aufgabe, Berlin

instance propagates the multi flat house with one central kitchen in particular with regard to similar benefits, which large factories are able to create economically.[38] Among those benefits for such a centralised production for private households without their own kitchens could be an increased division of labour by using the facilities of modern technology and technical means, savings on labour force and labour time including saving on capital investments per output unit, and savings on materials as a consequence of a more rational advantage taking. Furthermore there would be savings on rooms, cost-benefits as the result of purchasing by wholesale, increased leisure time and more intensive education of children through the members of such a centralised private household production being available for education, nursing, and other services.[39] Finally there would be a large substitution of female work in the isolated private households compared to the centralised private household production into the non-private household sectors, for instance in public service and private companies.

Friedrich Engels (1820-1895)[40]

August Bebel (1840-1913)[41]

In particular to release women from nearly all their engagements in private household production and their complete integration into the non-private household sectors, combined with the emancipation of women, with the claim of the transformation of private household production into forms of public organised

[38] Adolph (1919), p. 26

[39] Morgenstern, Lina (1900) Hilfsbuch zur Gründung, Leitung und Controle von Volksküchen; Kochrezepte der Berliner Volksküchen; Geschichte des Vereins von 1866-1900; Berlin, p. 12

[40] http://en.wikipedia.org/wiki/Friedrich_Engels

[41] http://en.wikipedia.org/wiki/August_Bebel

satisfaction of private needs, has to be seen as one of the fundamental goals of socialism.[42] *Friedrich Engels* declares the private household production as a part of the bourgeois society and their economic order, and he claims the abolishment of private household production to gain the economic benefits of the division of labour and importantly to realise the socialistic way of life. "The emancipation of women will be only possible if this occurs in the large scale production within the non-private household sectors and the private household production of women has been reduced to a negligible minimum. This has been made available through the modern large industry, which enables the labour of women on a large scale, but in the true sense demands the labour of women and furthermore also the private household production more and more dissolves into a public industry".[43] [44] *Engels* made his claim also in another part of the publication: "With the transformation of the means of production into social ownership the single family will be abolished as an economic unit of the society. The private household will be changed and integrated into a social industry".[45] [46] *Lenin* has a similar suggestion: "The true emancipation of women, the true communism will only succeed and begin, where and when the revolution (under the leadership of the governing proletariat) against this barbaric private household production or more convenient it would be if its large transformation into a socialistic large scale economy starts".[47][48] With regard to the emancipation of women *Lenin* comes up with the claim that women should be liberated from their slavery in their private households and to liberate her from her limited environment of kitchen and children's room as the main issue of the proletarian emancipation of women.[49]

Clara Zetkin expresses her ideas as such: "In short, we take it seriously with our programmatic claim to integrate the economic and educational functions of the sole private household into the society".[50] [51] Also *August Bebel* claims the abolishment of the private household production to achieve a large socialising of the various forms

---

42 Zetkin, Clara (1957) Für die Befreiung der Frau! Rede auf dem internationalen Arbeiterkongress zu Paris, 19. Juli 1889, in: Ausgewählte Reden und Schriften, Bd. 1, Berlin, pp. 4-5

43 Engels, Friedrich (1962) Der Ursprung der Familie, des Privateigentums und des Staates, in: Karl Marx/Friedrich Engels Werke, Band 21, Berlin, p. 158. This Treatise was published for the first time at Zürich in 1884.

44 Free translation made by the author.

45 ibid., p. 77

46 Free translation made by the author.

47 Lenin, Wladimir Iljitsch (1962) Die große Initiative, in: Werke, Bd. 29, Berlin, p. 419

48 Free translation made by the author.

49 Lenin, Wladimir Iljitsch (1961) Zum internationalen Frauentag (1920), in: Werke, Bd. 30, Berlin, p. 401

50 Zetkin, Clara (1926) Lenin ruft die werktätigen Frauen; Artikel Lenins zur Frauenfrage, Berlin, p. 36

51 Free translation made by the author.

of private household production: "The abolishment of the private kitchen will be for many women a relief. The private kitchen is an old-fashioned as well as an obsolete institution, in the same way as the workshop of the little master, both mean a large uneconomic inefficiency and a large waste of time, power, heating and illumination materials, nutritional material etc."[52] [53] *Braun* espoused the idea of the transformation of private household production into large living complexes in the sense of high rise towers of flats[54] under the conditions of a central state economy as the result of socialism.[55]

Clara Zetkin (1857-1933) and Rosa Luxemburg (1871-1919) [56] [57]

Contrary to the enthusiasm of the Socialists for the benefits of the industrialisation including the socialisation of the national economy and furthermore of their vision towards a progressive emancipation of women, the representatives of the bourgeois and middle class society, for instance *Schäffle* and *Morgenstern* only permit the transformation of parts of private household production into centralised

52 Bebel, August (1922) Die Frau und der Sozialismus, 50. Auflage, Stuttgart und Berlin, p. 469
53 Free translation made by the author.
54 Braun, Lilly (1901) Frauenarbeit und Hauswirtschaft, Berlin, pp. 21-22
55 ibid., p. 30
56 http://en.wikipedia.org/wiki/Clara_Zetkin
57 http://en.wikipedia.org/wiki/Rosa_Luxemburg

household production for people living in abnormal conditions, in times of war or in times of economic downturn.[58] Therefore their plan was basically limited to '*Volksküchen*' (public soup kitchens) and nursing homes. As an example of the establishment of public soup kitchens is the situation during WWI when, in the so called 'turnip winter' of 1917, approximately a quarter of the citizens in Hamburg had been provided with food in public soup kitchens.[59]

In a survey of 614 housewives across Germany (West) undertaken by the *Zentrale für Gasverwendung*, Frankfurt, in cooperation with the author in 1970, the interviewees were asked among others about their objections towards the visits to public soup kitchens: 77 interviewees (12.54%) had no objection, whereas 537 interviewees (87.46%) had objections in the sequence of first preference as inadequate quality (45.01%), second preference as too impersonal (43.83%), and third preference as remembrance on war and crisis (11.16%).[60]

1.2 Definition and Implementation of Private Household and Private Household Production within Economics

The rising economics at the end of the 19th century and its mathematical analysis with sets of equations for economic matters reduced the private household to an institution of sole consumption and the private household production was abolished due to the incapability to quantify the various household internal economic processes.[61] Economics of the 19th century is much more involved in the industrial progress and the establishment of a wider retail industry to provide an improved supply of goods and services as consumption for private households. This silent secularization occurred in the way that economics became a scientific discipline about the "laws" of the free market.[62] This process was based on the assumption

58 Schäffle, Albert (1896) Bau und Leben des socialen Körpers, 1. Bd., 2nd edition, 1st & 2nd volume, Tübingen, pp. 75-76
Morgenstern, Lina (1900) Hilfsbuch zur Gründung, Leitung und Controle von Volksküchen; Kochrezepte der Berliner Volksküchen; Geschichte des Vereins von 1866-1900, 3., erweiterte Aufl., nach 34 jähriger Erfahrung, Berlin, p. 10 & p. 12

59 Fürth, Henriette (1919) Gemeinwirtschaftliche Förderung der Haushaltung und der Lebenskraft, in: Schriften der Gesellschaft für Soziale Reform, Heft 69, Jena, pp. 20-21, dieselbe: Die Zentralküche als Kriegseinrichtung, in: Archiv für Sozialwissenschaft und Sozialpolitik, 41. Band, 2. Heft, Tübingen 1915, p. 470

60 Fischer, Wolfgang Chr. (1982) Entwicklung der privaten Hauswirtschaft, Baltmannsweiler, p. 114

61 Reichenau, Charlotte von (1943) Die Hauswirtschaft als Produktion und die Wissenschaft, in: Hauswirtschaftliche Jahrbücher, 16. Jg., Heft 2, Stuttgart, p. 90

62 Lütge, Friedrich (1966) Deutsche Sozial- und Wirtschaftsgeschichte, Ein Überblick, dritte, wesentlich vermehrte und verbesserte Auflage, Berlin-Heidelberg-New York, p. 412

that economics could orientate on the methods of the natural science, incorporating the ideal of exactitude and the measuring to obtain precise solutions to market related processes, for instance analyses of competition, monopolies, cartels, duopolies, oligopolies, and perfect competition. "Three economics texts from the late 1890s – by *Gustav Schmoller* (Germany), *Herbert Foxwell* (UK), and *Thorstein Veblen* (US) – represent the revolt against formalism and the resulting taming of capitalism. Although their styles and agendas were different, they are important representatives of the alternative theory that solidified on both sides of the Atlantic during the 1890s. They created an alternative to what *Gustav Schmoller* called *the irrational twins: Manchester Liberalism* and communism. This 1890s generation laid the foundations for the Middle Way between communism and *Manchester liberalism*, for a regulated capitalism with decent economic distribution and after the 1930s – as long as this theory was kept in place – also without major financial crises."[63]

Thorstein Bunde Veblen (1857-1929)[64]

On the other hand the more historical and juridical orientated economics, the so-called 'institutionalism' or the 'German historical school' or the 'Verein für Socialpolitik', was regarded as a minor discipline of economics. The economic process within private households has no more any place within economics because any economic activity has its final end at the 'door' of private households. The term 'household management' became at this stage exclusively the meaning of a rational allocation of household goods and services and after the purchasing of consumptive

63 Reinert (2013), p. 59

64 http://en.wikipedia.org/wiki/Thorsten_Veblen

goods and services there is only the process of pure consumption and nothing more. The private households have not any more productive functions and activities; they have been transformed into an economic institution, which has been stripped of its various internal activities and been degraded to a pure unit of consumption.[65] This scientific view about the household production continues into the 20th century and a minority of economists like *Erich Egner* and *Fritz W. Meyer* are opposing this limited notion of the private household and its productive activities as unrealistic.[66]

Fritz W. Meyer (1907-1980)[67]

[65] Lexis, Wilhelm (1907) Konsumtion, in: Wörterbuch der Volkswirtschaft, 2. Band, zweite, völlig umgearbeitete Auflage, Jena, p. 296 and 298

[66] Meyer, Fritz W. (1967) Die Haushaltung in der Nationalökonomie, in: ORDO, Jahrbuch für die Ordnung von Wirtschaft und Gesellschaft, Bd. XVIII, Düsseldorf-München, pp. 279-298
Meyer, Fritz W. (1960) Was bedeutet „Regulation" für die Teilzahlunggsbanken, in: Festschrift zum zehnjährigen Bestehen der Mittelrheinischen Kundenkreditbank, Dr. Horbach & Co., K. G., Neuwied, p. 45
Egner, Erich (1958) Eigenart und Aufgabe hauswirtschaftlicher Forschung, in: Zeitschrift für die gesamte Staatswissenschaft, 114. Band, Tübingen, p. 258

[67] Private photo by the author at Prof. Meyer's garden party at his home in the 70s

In the middle of the twentieth century economics in Germany was dominated by the market orientated private household without any productive functions. For instance *Wilhelm Krelle* defines the private household as such: "households are economic units, which have no original production of goods".[68] [69] *Krelle* defines the private household production very rigorously as "because nothing is produced there and therefore there is no basic production, production functions and cost functions do not exist".[70] [71] Much more realistic seems to be the scientific position of *Erich Egner*, who implements the private household into a broader economic analysis and considers the private household as a socio-economic institution, which depends on the social and economic development within an economy.[72] His definition of the private household is orientated primarily on safeguarding the livelihood of the household members, which means that the two sides of the livelihood are the providing of means and the utilisation of means.[73] This concept of *Egner* is opposed to the concept of the free market with private households without productive activities and private companies and their maximum profit-taking.[74]

The *private household* can be defined as "a social economic institution which encompasses socially a social institution and economically an economic institution, with the objective to satisfy the needs of the household members".[75] [76] Furthermore the institution of *private household production* can be defined as "the household production as the production area of the private household encloses all measures with the intention to provide goods and services to the private final consumption".[77] [78]

Nevertheless the value of private household production within the accountancy of the *Gross Domestic Product* (GDP) of a national economy is by its concept completely neglected world-wide. The protagonists [79] of honouring private household production have the long standing request for its implementation in the

---

68 Free translation made by the author.
69 Krelle, Wilhelm (1961) Preistheorie, Tübingen-Zürich, p. 108
70 Free translation made by the author.
71 Krelle (1961), p. 108
72 Egner, Erich (1952) Der Haushalt, Eine Darstellung seiner volkswirtschaftlichen Gestalt, Berlin, p. 30
73 ibid., p. 27
74 Egner, Erich (1956) Haushalt, in: Handwörterbuch der Sozialwissenschaften, 5. Band, Göttingen, p. 66
75 Free translation made by the author.
76 Fischer (1982), p. 30
77 Free translation made by the author.
78 Fischer (1982), p. 30
79 Mostly representatives of the Domestic Science and Home Economics

GDP. There has been often quoted the humorous comparison: "When a Professor marries his household maid then the GDP declines".

1.3 Private Household Production and Economic Division of Labour

One can identify within the private household production and economic division of labour three major subject matters with regard to the integration of the private household production into the development of an economy.[80] These three subject matters are: *Industrialisation of private household production, Mechanisation of private household production,* and *Centralisation of private household production.*

The *Industrialisation* of the private household production takes place in the trend of the industrial development through the improving process of the division of labour within an economy. Some private household production functions are transferred to the market and private companies are able to produce these former activities within the private household with a much more economical mass production and the involved benefits of the economies of scale. To which extent the transfer of some private household production functions into the market occurs depends on:

- the amount of costs for such a production either in the private household or in the private companies by considering the possibility to rationalise these productions;
- the technical production possibilities within the private household;
- the situation in the labour force, in particular for female part-time employment;
- the private household income;
- the stage of the possibility to produce goods and services for private households within the market;
- the employment opportunities of the members of the private household;
- the location of the private household, in particular in consideration of the degree of the self-sufficiency with natural resources like domestic animals, fruit and vegetables;
- the extent of the individuality of the goods and services required for the private consumption;
- the activity of the government's policies with regard to the private household production.[81]

---

[80] See for specific details Fischer (1982), pp. 69-122

[81] Fischer (1982), p. 77

The *Mechanisation* of the private household production appears as the household orientated production of goods and services for the private consumption with the support of a set of machines with technically improved efficiency. [82] The mechanisation of the private household production in the wake of the industrialisation leads to a substitution of private labour force through capital in the form of labour-saving machines that means a transformation from labour-intensive to capital-intensive production on the basis of technical progress. To which extent the transfer of some private household production functions into the market occurs depends on:

- the amount of costs for such a production either in the private household or in the private companies by considering the possibility to rationalise the production of labour-saving machines;
- the amount of household income;
- the situation in the labour force market;
- the leisure time possibilities;
- the standard of living;
- the grade of mechanisation of other private households production;
- the stages of life and the size of private households;
- the state of engineering of machines for private households use;
- the financial possibilities to purchase machines, for example leasing of machines and hire purchasing of machines for private household production;
- the activity of the government's policies with regard to the private household production.[83] [84]

The *Mechanisation* of private household production took place mostly at the turn of the twentieth century when machines were developed for large households in the first place rather than for small sized households. A typical example would be the refrigeration of foodstuffs for restaurants, canteens, and large sized households. The technical development of smaller units for refrigeration was developed after WWI and much more improved after WWII. Through various forms of marketing starting

---

82 See to the development of sets of machines for the private household production: Giedion, Siegfried (1948) Mechanization takes command; a contribution to anonymous history; New York.
Fourastié, Jean (1962) Machinisme et Bien-Etre; Niveau de vie et genre de vie en France de 1700 à nos jours, Paris, p. 220

83 Fischer (1982), p. 93
Fischer, Wolfgang Chr. (1978) Aspekte der Einflußnahme privater Haushalte auf die Kollektiv-güterversorgung, in: Hauswirtschaft und Wissenschaft, Heft 3, München, pp. 108-111

84 For example: the Federal German Government subsidized and granted the mechanization of farm households through financial assistance provided by the Ministry of Agriculture in the 1950s and 1960s in West-Germany.

already in the 1950s and 1960s the main goal of companies producing machines for private household production like refrigerators, washing machines, dishwashers, microwave ovens, vacuum cleaners and home entertainment units was to convince consumers to live in small sized private households.[85] The three or four generation private household disappeared successively with the industrialisation and mechanisation of private households and elderly people were shifted to some form of centralised private households like nursing homes and serviced apartments.[86]

The Troubled Household in the early 19th century[87]

---

[85] See Appendix 1.

[86] Bielfeld, Gretha (1930) Die Mechanisierung des Haushalts und ihre volkswirtschaftliche Bedeutung, in: Veröffentlichung des Instituts für Hauswirtschaftswissenschaft an der Akademie für soziale und pädagogische Frauenarbeit in Berlin, Heft 6, Langensalza
Seeberg, Stella (1967) Langlebige Haushaltsgüter und Haushaltsinvestitionen, in: Aspekte des hauswirtschaftlichen Strukturwandels, in: Beiträge zue Ökonomie von Haushalt und Verbrauch, Heft 3, Berlin
Meyer-Pollack, Erna (1915) Der Haushalt eines höheren Beamten in den Jahren 1880-1906; untersucht an Hand von Wirtschaftsrechnungen; in: Schriften des Vereins für Sozialpolitik, 145. Bd., München-Leipzig
Plassmann, Christa (1969) Die Investitionsleistungen der privaten Haushalte in der BRD; in: Die Finanzen des privaten Haushalts; Festschrift für Walter Kaminsky; Frankfurt

[87] Jacobus Josephus Eeckhout (Belgian Painter 1793-1861), Wikimedia Commons

Dutch Household (second half of 16th century)[88]

The *Centralisation* of private household production and its integration into the economic development has been a long standing political plea of some socialist groups to abolish private household production and liberate women from their historical household chores through centralised household production in large living complexes.[89] Apart from the economies of scale through mass production and personnel employed in such complexes, including some improvement in social life, there are some disadvantages such as:

- minor possibility of centralisation by decentralised local settlement;
- neglecting more specialised individual demand for goods and services for private consumption in particular in the section of food preparation;
- possibility of wasting materials, energy, and maintenance of large machines through a reduced personal responsibility of employees in the centralised household;
- neglecting the possibility to enjoy private household production functions as a means of spending leisure time, for example cooking as a hobby;
- establishment of a large administration and control management;

88 Gillis Mostaert (1528–1598), Wikimedia Commons.
89 Bebel (1922), p. 469

– intense dependence of the individual on non-private household institutions;
– possibility of the destruction of the family as a preferred unit of the society.

A comparison of the economic advantages and disadvantages of the centralisation of the private household production can be seen as problematic because even a comparison of the quality of the goods and services provided by different private households is nearly impossible. Whether the centralisation of private household production is established on a large scale is a question of political intentions.[90]

One form of the *Centralisation* of the private household production, that is the *soup kitchens* and *workhouses*, had been established a few centuries ago, in particular for impoverished people through the churches or other welfare institutions. A soup kitchen, a bread line, or a meal centre is a place where food is offered to the hungry for free or at a reasonably low price. Frequently located in lower-income neighbourhoods, they are often staffed by volunteer organizations, such as church groups or community groups. Soup kitchens sometimes obtain food from a food bank for free or at a low price, because they are considered a charity which makes it easier for them to feed the many people who visit the soup kitchen.[91] It is believed the term 'breadline', entered the popular lexicon in the 1880s. It was during those years that a noteworthy bakery in New York City's Greenwich Village, 'Fleischmann Model Viennese Bakery', instituted a policy of distributing unsold baked goods to the poor at the end of their business day. The concept of soup kitchens hit the mainstream of United States consciousness during the *Great Depression* in the 1920s and 1930s. One soup kitchen in Chicago was even sponsored by American mobster Al Capone in an effort to clean up his image. Inventor Benjamin Thompson, contemporary to the Founding Fathers of the United States, is said to have invented the soup kitchen.[92]

---

[90] See in detail trials for centralisation in the former German Democratic Republic: Gericke, Hans-Jürgen: Der Einfluβ einer rationellen Organisation der Konsumtion in hauswirtschaftlichen Bereich auf die effektive Gestaltung der gesellschaftlichen Produktion.
Keck, Alfred und Manz, Günter (1967) neue Aspekte der Planung der nichtproduktiven Konsumtion, in: Beiträge zur Lebensstandardforschung, Schriftenreihe Planung und Leitung der Volks-wirtschaft, Berlin.
Rössler, Hans (1967) Die Konsumtion als Faktor des Wirtschaftswachstums, in: Die Konsumtion im Reproduktionsprozeβ, Beiträge zur sozialistischen Konsumtionsforschung, Bd. 2, Wissen-schaftliche Beiträge der Martin-Luther-Universität Halle-Wittenberg, Halle-Wittenberg.
[91] http://en.wikipedia.org/wiki/Soup_kitchen, accessed 27th February 2012
[92] ibid.

Soup Kitchen Maryborough, Queensland, Australia 2009[93]

Members of the United States Navy serve the homeless at Dorothy's Soup Kitchen in August 2009, Salinas, California[94]

---

93 Photograph made by the author in Maryborough

94 Photograph in Wikipedia article "Soup Kitchen"

Volunteers of America Soup Kitchen in Washington, D.C. in 1936[95]

[95] Photograph in Wikipedia article "Soup Kitchen".

Chapter 2

-------ꝏ------

Private Household Production and Free Market Regime

This chapter is intended to analyse the integration of private household production into the economy according to the three forms. The *industrialisation* of private household production seems to be the dominant form and the *mechanisation* of private household production has reached a grade of saturation, which can be shown on the equipment of private households with technical goods. Only the *mechanisation* has some further opportunities within the home entertainment goods like TV, audio, computers etcetera. The *centralisation* of private household production seems to be reduced to mainly for elderly people and their specific needs according to their lifestyle and according to their health in certain households like nursing homes and serviced apartments. This shift of former private household activities, in the sense that the young family is caring for the elderly, is a typical sign of a disintegration of a society. This development has its origin, among other factors, in the propagation of independent households wherever and whenever possible in the interest of *mechanising* and *industrialising* private household production.

2.1 Consumer Sovereignty and Free Market Economy

Paul Davies recalls in his book 'The Eerie Silence – Are We Alone in the Universe?' in the year 2010: "Accurate as of London, circa 1960, for those who are interested. My best friend Brian was the milkman's son, and would occasionally help his father with deliveries. He even recalls turning out on Christmas Day, such was the level of service in the Good Old Days. The milk bottles were originally conveyed to the customer on a horse-drawn cart, and the horse would often get a carrot as a Christmas present. Then the horses were decommissioned in favour of a soulless electrical vehicle. Then the milkman himself was decommissioned, along with the bottles and the vehicle, in favour of horrid supermarket cartons. Such is progress."[96] But this has changed within a few decades substantially: today the workforce has become so called 'flexible' and more and more people looking for work are facing either unemployment or just some contracts to be on call. In the *Sun Community Newspapers*[97], was published an advertisement for an Ergon Energy call centre. In particular the following sentence seems to be remarkable: "As a casual employee your hours will vary from week to week, dependent on business requirements and call volumes, allowing you the flexibility to still enjoy all the extra things in life". Welcome to the journeyman, the day-worker of the 18th century and before. Meanwhile one can make some 'fun' about the industrial reserve army and these casual employed workers have to seek for further income, maybe for another on call employment hoping the times they were needed don't clash. But where is the possibility of these people to produce something useful for their consumption as household production, and where is a way for planning a relatively secured future? Long leisure time with all the temptation to forget the reality with alcohol, drugs etcetera and the search for money becomes the *ultima ratio*, not the worries about the weather for their plants and the welfare of their domestic animals around the house.

Social imbalance should be according to *Kurt Rothschild* a "challenge for economics to get more involved in social problems, when we consider the almost paradoxical experience, contrary to many economists' expectations, that even in the developed industrial countries the socio-economic problems have not really decreased, despite the rapid rise of social wealth due to science and technology."[98] With regard to the economy ethics should not be dismissed as irrelevant, nor should the sole concern be material goods and consumption: human values, such as the possibility of being in the paid workforce or simply the retention of dignity as a human being are just as important. *Sebastian Haffner* summarized the way a modern state is shaped by pursuing a certain *Conception of State:* 'It is clear that at the heart of every political doctrine there lies not a policy but a philosophy – this is certainly true of Germany. What inwardly divides Liberals, Conservatives, and Socialists is a different vision of mankind. The different conceptions of the State are merely the outcome. The differences arise from the fact that each party wishes to construct the State in a way that shall approximate as closely as possible to their conception of mankind that shall favour their human ideal. At a still later stage is shaped the concrete political programme, according to which the State is to be constructed and

[96] Davies, Paul (2010)
[97] Sun Community Newspapers (2013) March 20, Townsville, p. 40
[98] Rothschild (1992), p. 49

safeguarded..."[99] This applies certainly to policies Governments are engaged in to shape *Consumer Affairs.*

The very existence of *Consumer Affairs* as a concern is an admission of the failure of *Consumer Sovereignty*, which means in short that consumers in the economy determine the production of goods and services by casting money 'votes'. Traditional rational consumers (so-called *'homo economicus'*) consistently make optimum decisions, as they are perfectly informed about the prices and all characteristics of all products and services for sale. The theory behind this *'homo economicus'* sets the conditions under which the consumer maximises his satisfaction from a given budget and is able to identify whether one parcel of goods and services is preferable to another. These assumptions of consumer behaviour lead to the *'Law of demand'*, stating that the quantity of products and services purchased is inversely related only to the price. Of course, this holds only in theory. In the course of time it has been proven beyond doubt that the old fashioned (and related) concept of *Caveat Emptor* (sold as seen) has been denied for decades.[100] It is indisputable that market failure relating to the lack of sufficient information about price, quality, durability, availability, time and environmental performance of consumer goods and services exists. Consumer organizations in OECD countries agree that consumers do not have the collective power to make relevant changes in the marketplace, and not at all in remote areas. Consumers are not sovereign, this being a fiction as income is unevenly distributed; there is a lack of sufficient information about price, availability and quality performance of goods and services; and the widespread rise of marketing and the associated use of sophisticated techniques in selling products and services. The notion of the equality of bargaining positions is also most unlikely.[101]

Within *Economics* since the 18th century, especially during the period of the classics and the so called marginal benefit theory, it was persistently assumed that consumers made rational purchasing decisions as a result of underlying rational behaviour. Since the 20th Century this has been challenged by, amongst others, the studies of *Thorstein Veblen (1857-1929)* and his famous book *'Theory of the leisure class'*, and *George Katona* and his numerous publications on consumer behaviour. It has since become obvious that beside economic factors like price, quality, durability, availability, time and environmental aspects, sociological and psychological factors are crucial. Furthermore *Maynes* asserts that *John Kenneth Galbraith* in his renowned

99 Haffner, Sebastian (2008) Germany Jekyll and Hyde, An eyewitness analysis of Nazi Germany, with an introduction by Neal Ascherson, Abacus, London, p. 179

100 Fischer & Massey (1994b), p. 294

101 ibid.

book *'The Affluent Society'* stands almost alone among economists in stressing the role of advertising in creating and managing the preferences of consumers.[102]

In attacking the received doctrines of economics, *Galbraith* stresses two major themes:
1. *Producers, Not Consumers, Are Sovereign.*
Through successful advertising and salesmanship, producers/sellers 'manage' the preferences of consumers. Thus, it is producers, not consumers, who ultimately determine the volume and composition of output.
2. *Many of the Wants Being Satisfied in Our Economy Are Nonurgent, even Frivolous.*
This follows from the notion that many wants are contrived by sellers and are not original with consumers themselves.[103]

Basically and in a broader sense it should be conceded that *Galbraith* is right. With regard to *Consumer Protection* it might be said that "law reflects the spirit of the people whose law it is; and on the other hand that the laws are merely a superficial growth on an economic structure dictated by the will of the ruling class. In a modern pluralist society such as Australia, the truth probably lies between the two extremes".[104] *Goldring* asserts that "the need for legal regulation of the activities of those who deal with consumers arises from the small minority of unscrupulous or reckless people who are not prepared to accept responsibility for the goods and services they provide."[105]

If we concede that *Galbraith* is right, the imbalance between corporate sellers and consumers could be seen in the following way: "The individual private consumer is typically an amateur dealing with a highly skilled professional, and will, also typically, lack the skill, knowledge, awareness or even the incentive (in respect to small transactions) to attempt to act as would the professional."[106] Furthermore, it might be said that consumers are not interested in goods as such, but in their properties or characteristics. Thus, the individual's constrained choice involves both the spaces of characteristics and the space of goods, linked through the consumption technology. Individual preferences determine the relative weights given to the various characteristics in making choices, and thus different individuals

[102] Maynes (1976), p. 263
[103] ibid.
[104] Goldring (1987), p. 1
[105] ibid, p. 7
[106] Terry (1988), p. 123

may choose different goods or collections of goods even though they face a common consumption technology.[107]

Consumer behaviour may be defined as the decision process and physical activity individuals engage in when evaluating, acquiring, using or disposing of goods and services.[108] Consumer behaviour involves a mental decision process as well as physical activity. Therefore the act of purchase is just one part of the decision process, and remains part of a system of mental and physical activities that occur during a period of time. Some of these activities precede the actual buying, while others follow it. It is noteworthy that factors affecting individuals in their daily lives also influence their purchase activities. Internal influences, such as learning and motives, as well as external factors, such as social expectations and constraints, affect consumer behaviour.[109] Moreover consumer behaviour is enfold in culture, that is everything socially learned and shared by the members of a society as ideas, customs, beliefs and habits.[110] *William J McGuire* identified sixteen major motivational influences:

1. *Consistency.* Motivation to maintain a coherent and organised view of the world. Example: Learning that the cereal we considered nutritious really is not very high in food value, and consequently feeling 'uncomfortable' and attempting to find an explanation for this inconsistency.
2. *Attribution.* Motivation to understand or infer causes for various occurrences. This is focused in three major directions: inferences as to the causes of various events; attempts to understand our own attitudes, values and so on from the behaviour we see ourselves engaging in; and inferences about the reasons other people act the way they do. Example: the meaning we derive from information in our environment, such as promotional messages, being strongly influenced by attribution inferences.
3. *Categorisation.* Motivation to categorise complex information in order to organise and deal with it more easily. Example: Dividing clothing into formal, casual and 'hang-around' categories.
4. *Objectification.* Motivation to use 'objective', external information instead of internal reflection to draw conclusions about our values, attitudes and the like. This is similar to attribution but more passive in nature. Example: Using the amount of ski equipment purchased as a measure of the degree we enjoy the sport.

---

107 Lancaster (1991), p. 4
108 Lawson (1996), p. 4
109 ibid., p. 7
110 ibid., p. 74

5. *Autonomy.* Motivation to seek individuality and personal growth through self-actualisation and development of a distinct identity. Example: reading various self-help books in order to improve ourselves.
6. *Exploration.* Motivation to seek stimulation through new events or circumstances. Example: Impulse buying or switching from favourite to other brands to generate some excitement in our lives.
7. *Matching.* Motivation to develop mental images of ideal situations and regularly compare (match) perceptions of actual situations to these ideals. A strong matching motive implies that internal standards, not characteristics of other brands, are more important criteria for judging products. Example: Comparing a new car model to our ideal car rather than to other brands.
8. *Utilitarian.* Motivation to use the external environment as a valuable resource for information and skills to help solve life's problems. Example: Doing a lot of 'window shopping' to see how available products can help around the home.
9. *Tension reduction.* Motivation to reduce or avoid any tension that is generated when needs are not being satisfied. Example: Avoiding new brands because they generate uncertainty (and tension) regarding how well they will perform.
10. *Self-expression.* Motivation to project our identities to others. Example: Purchasing an Alpha Romeo Spider to reflect our enjoyment of the sporty life in the fast lane.
11. *Ego-defensive.* Motivation to protect ourselves from social embarrassment and other threats to feelings of self-worth. Example: Purchasing underarm deodorant, dandruff shampoo, strong denture adhesive or carpet freshener to avoid the potential of social disgrace.
12. *Reinforcement.* Motivation to act in ways that have previously resulted in rewarding situations. Example: Consistently arguing with the car mechanic because such behaviour was necessary in the past to get the car fixed properly.
13. *Assertion.* Motivation to strive for competition, power and success. Example: Using some products, such as the latest software, to get ahead of the pack.
14. *Affiliation.* Motivation to seek acceptance, affection and warm personal contact with others. Example: Becoming a member of a service organisation such as Lions or Rotary.
15. *Identification.* Motivation to develop new identities and roles to enhance our self-concepts. Acting these roles out in social settings allows expression of values and development of feelings of importance. Example: Patronising certain 'gathering spots' frequented by young professionals in an attempt to belong or identify with that group.

16. *Modelling.* Motivation to imitate other individuals with whom we identify or empathise. Example: Buying G.I. Joe, Rambo, Gladiators or similar toys.[111]

Cultural values in Australia and in many OECD countries are undergoing some major changes. Some researchers believe that many of these trends have had the effect of fragmenting social groups and breaking down the sense of social cohesion in society. *Mackay* identified seven major aspects related to his studies in Australia:[112]

1. The struggle between men and women over the redefinition of gender roles has led, for the time being, to a cautious, more adversarial approach to relationships between the sexes, replacing our traditional acceptance of pair bonding as the basis of our social structure with greater emphasis on the individual.
2. The rising divorce rate has fragmented family life to an extent that has forced many Australians to search - often fruitlessly - outside a family for a group, a herd, a tribe to which they might belong.
3. The 'personal growth' movement, which gained so much momentum during the 1970s and 1980s, encouraged egocentricity and, for many people, led to an obsession with personal gratification to the exclusion of traditional concepts of social cohesion.
4. Multiculturalism has seemed, in the short term, to place more emphasis on diversity than unity.
5. Politics has become virtually synonymous with economics and, in the process, has seemed to many Australians to have retreated from a concern for human values and social justice.
6. In corporate life, information technology has become so sophisticated that data transfer is often confused with communication, and personal relationships within organisations have suffered directly as a result. Sending and receiving disembodied information is increasingly allowed to occupy time that used to be spent in keeping closely in touch with each other.
7. On the domestic front, technology has played its part in fragmenting the herd: the dishwasher replaces an episode of personal interaction during washing up; the microwave oven reduces the need for the family to eat at the same time.

It would be unrealistic to argue that consumers in *Western Societies* are uniform or have a similar range of attitudes to private consumption. More or less since the late 1960s, after the so-called *'Hippie Movement'* that originated firstly in *San Francisco/California*, *Western Societies* have become split into different groups. The greater part of *Western Societies*, including the Australian society, are composed of

---

[111] Lawson (1996), pp. 317-318, based on William J McGuire (1976) Some Internal Psychological Factors Influencing Consumer Choice, Journal of Consumer Research 2, March, pp. 302-19

[112] ibid., pp. 99-100

those people in the work force with sufficient income and assets, who are willing to adjust their standard of living from time to time, but who basically have prospects of long term improvement, and are encouraged by the ideal of a market economy giving everybody a fair chance to achieve a comfortable standard of living. Their political views towards unemployed persons and welfare beneficiaries are that they are necessary and that they are reasonable to support. However they are convinced that the market economy has a built-in self-regulation system and that economic growth and technical progress will benefit future standards of living in the long term. [113] On the other hand sometimes they are victims of so-called 'passive consumption'. Examples being the 'consumption' of goods such as video games, the over-utilisation of television, dreaming of future holidays, gambling, and filling the loneliness and emotional emptiness with consumer goods and services. More often today, unlike preceding generations, young couples have the intention to immediately set up their household with a range of new appliances, rather than improvising, or utilising inherited or second-hand goods, looking for donations or producing their own goods, and thus by-passing the gradual accumulation period of household goods, as performed by older generations. The more recent generations who have matured after the world depression of the 1930s and after WWII, have not experienced the hardship the majority of people of preceding generations in Australia and other OECD countries experienced. Hence, their willingness to increase private consumption, compared to the elderly generation has vastly increased, due to the change in attitude towards affordable consumption.

Contrary to this, there are the so-called *'drop-out' groups*, or people who mistrust the advantages and benefits of the 'glamorous facade' of consumption within western societies, remaining unconvinced of the ultimate solution of the market economy for the sake of people. They do not trust politicians to solve social and economic problems like high unemployment, misery and poverty, and rely mostly on their own abilities. Most likely, this part of western society is looking for a niche in which they can live, with an adjusted standard of living back to an emotional, creative, independent and environmentally adjusted mode of behaviour which enables them to live simply without the pressure of a 'must have' consumption-style. This does not mean that these people are neglecting some advantages of modern development, but it is a quite different lifestyle, which has often led, particularly in the 1970s, to them being categorised as non-conformist strangers, or sometimes miscellaneous fugitives.

---

[113] Fischer (1984), p. 96

Overall, one has to bear in mind that "through changing living conditions today at the end of the 20th century, human beings are again and again being challenged as it was the case in medieval Europe at the beginning of the period of industrialisation."[114] When the daily life was much more uncomplicated than in modern times, people sold and bought goods with a minimum of legal intervention. Consumer affairs were based on the principle of *'caveat emptor'*, that means 'let the buyer beware'. "In an era when people lived in small; closely knit communities, when goods were made by hand, usually by someone who lived nearby and who was known to the community, such a principle worked quite well and, on the whole, it wasn't as harsh as it might seem on the surface."[115] Inspection of goods carefully before buying had been an option for customers and often the word spread quickly about a manufacturer or seller who deceived, with obvious ramifications for the future viability of the business.[116]

As a result of expanded division of labour and enhanced automation the daily life of consumers became more complicated when the industrialisation started. Consumers faced more and more sophisticated products and services than within the eras before and purchasing products and services required legal support. This was mainly based on three major determinants:

1. Manufacturers and consumers became gradually more distant from one another with limited or no personal connection at all, for instance with regard to the establishment of large transnational companies. It may be demonstrated by the large size of the main European retailers, whereas like Australia and New Zealand the whole retail sectors are primarily controlled by two or three major companies.
2. The rapid development of technology made it impossible for consumers to examine sufficiently products and services due to a lack of knowledge. In particular after WWII *'planned obsolescence'* forced consumers to purchase deliberately inferior products to keep the industry engaged.
3. New marketing strategies including sophisticated advertising were developed to convince consumers of their so-called 'needs', creating a business environment in which sometimes misleading and fraudulent business practices disadvantaged individual consumers.

When introducing the *Trade Practices Bill* into the Australian Parliament in 1973 the Attorney-General Senator the Hon *L K Murphy* QC argued: "In consumer transactions unfair practices are widespread. The existing law is still founded on the

---

114 Richarz (1992), p. 44
115 Healey (1995), p. 1
116 ibid., p. 2

principle known as caveat emptor meaning 'let the buyer beware'. That principle may have been appropriate for transactions conducted in village markets. It has ceased to be appropriate as a general rule. Now the marketing of goods and services is conducted on an organized basis and by trained business executives. The untrained consumer is no match for the businessman who attempts to persuade the consumer to buy goods or services on terms and conditions suitable to the vendor. The consumer needs protection by the law and this Bill will provide such protection."[117]

The United States made the first move in the area of consumer protection. President *John F Kennedy* delivered in March 1962 the first '*Declaration of Consumer Rights*' to the United States Congress:

1. *The right to safety* - to be protected against the marketing of goods that are hazardous to health or life.
2. *The right to be informed* - to be protected against fraudulent, deceitful, or grossly misleading information, advertising, labelling, and other practices, and to be given the facts needed to make informed choices.
3. *The right to choose* - to be assured, wherever possible, access to a variety of products and services at competitive prices, and in those industries in which competition is not workable and government regulation is substituted, there should be assurance of satisfactory quality and service at fair prices.
4. *The right to be heard* - to be assured that consumer interests will receive full and sympathetic consideration in the formulation of government policy and fair and expeditious treatment in its administrative tribunals.[118]

The growth of *Consumer Affairs* has been encouraged since *Ralph Nader* published his attack on the US motor vehicle industry '*Unsafe at Any Speed*' in 1965. In particular, the 'right to be informed' indicates a failure in the provision of proper market information to consumers. This is not only related to consumer goods and services but also to services provided by financial institutions, espousing the consumers' right to receive proper, clearly understandable information about 'invisible' products like credit. It might be argued that "legislation is necessary to enforce standards of market behaviour, and the existence of effective legislation and consumer protection authorities creates an awareness of the rights of consumers throughout the community."[119] *Swan* has asserted that "to suggest that the consumer can be fully protected by regulations during a continual process of evolutionary

---

[117] Goldring (1987), p. 2
[118] Troelstrup (1974), p. 23
[119] Goldring (1987), p. 4

change is of course complete nonsense."[120] Nevertheless, this might lead to questions about the costs of regulation rather than to the principal issue of social obligations to consumers who failed in managing their private consumption and their private credit properly.[121]

However there is among the scientific community a challenge to the traditional view of mainstream economics about the human brain and its various implications for human behavior. "The brain physiology research of leading evolutionary neuroscientist, *Paul MacLean*, has important implications for human economic motivation. *Gerald Cory* in his research has admirably utilized *MacLean*'s findings and has persuasively explained that humans have two dominant motivations: 1) ego or self-interest and 2) empathy or other-interest, which our brains attempt to balance. This view is clearly important and at odds with mainstream economics in which self-interest is the dominant motivation."[122] The MacLean-Cory view, also known as *Dual Motive Theory* represents a serious challenge to mainstream economics. However, the *Dual Motive Theory* leaves something to be desired. Accordingly, the purpose is to revise *Dual Motive Theory* utilizing the *Concept of Brain Plasticity* and it is argued that the mainstream economic image of the brain is not supported by current knowledge of brain science. "*Brain Plasticity* refers to the ability of the brain to change structurally and functionally as a result of input from the environment. Some of this plasticity is no doubt genetically determined but some brain change is a product of individual effort and represents the individual's investment in intangible capital (standard human capital, social capital, personal capital, and so on). In this revised view, the balance that individuals, groups, and societies strike between ego and empathy orientation is to a great extent determined by these intangible investments, not simply by brain physiology."[123]

It is interesting how human beings act in times of an economic downfall, that is in a situation of substantial misery, distress, poverty and loss of dignity. The play 'Saint Joan of the Stockyards', written by *Bertold Brecht* between 1929 and 1931 seems to have still a quite remarkable relevance for today.[124] Johanna is a Lieutenant of the '*Black Straw Hats*' (Leutnant der Schwarzen Strohhüte) in Chicago during the World Depression of 1929. In this version of the story of Joan of Arc, Brecht transforms her into 'Joan Dark', a member of the 'Black Straw Hats' (a Salvation Army-like group) in 20th-century Chicago. The play charts Joan's battle with Pierpont Mauler,

---

[120] Swan (1987), p. 12
[121] Fischer & Massey (1994b), p. 295
[122] Tomer (2012)
[123] ibid.
[124] Brecht (1962)

the unctuous owner of a meat-packing plant. Like her predecessor, Joan is a doomed woman, a martyr and (initially, at least) an innocent in a world of strike-breakers, fat cats, and penniless workers. Within the play Joan focuses on the important question about the moral of poor people. "Joan: Why is this misery in the world? Well how should it be different! Of course if everyone bashes the next one on the head with an axe just to obtain a piece of ham for their bread which the victim needed for his survival as well as the attacker, if a brother is wrestling to obtain the absolute necessary minimum, how should not the sense for the almighty be extinct. ...My gentlemen I always am informed that poor people do not have enough morals and this is the case. Down there in the slums there is breeding the amoral by itself and subsequently the revolution. But I ask you: From where should they have a moral if they don't have anything else? Yes where to take if not to steal? My gentlemen there exists also a moral purchasing power. Lift the moral purchasing power then you have the total moral. And I mean with purchasing power something very simple and natural and that is money wages. And this leads me again to the reality: If you go ahead like before then you could gobble your own meat by yourself at the end because those outside (on the place of the slaughterhouses) they have no purchasing power."[125]

Jessie Street notably described the devastating effects of the *World Depression* in the 1930s in Australia: "For Australia's economy at the end of 1930, all was far from well. The fatal cut of 10 per cent in federal award wages and all government salaries, ordered by the Bank of England emissaries Sir Otto Niemeyer and Professor TE Gregory, quickly brought about the inevitable and disastrous consequences. The reduction of purchasing power resulting from the reduction of salaries and wages was further undermining the economy and more and more people lost their jobs and joined the unemployed. Manufacturers and businesses cut their staff, adding to the distress. Newspaper reports showed the numbers of unemployed still increasing and as those thrown out of work received only a small sustenance payment, many families were unable to pay their rent. Crisis followed crisis as people were evicted from their homes with nowhere to go. When I drove my car one day to see the reality behind the constant news of evictions, I saw for myself the forcible removal of families. In front of one closed house a woman was sitting on a chair with a child in her lap; there was a cot with another child standing up in it and another child sitting on the edge of the pavement. They were surrounded by their few household goods not already sold. Shanty towns sprang up around Sydney with those evicted making shelters of pieces of timber, old boxes or beaten-out kerosene tins."[126]

---

125 Free translation of page 52 by the author of this chapter

126 Coltheart (2004), p. 79

Furthermore *Jessie Street* doubted that capitalism as a desired social and economic order may be appropriate to solve such a tremendous crisis as the *World Depression* from the end of the 1920s to the beginning of WWII in 1939. "It was beyond my comprehension that empty houses and food were destroyed, while children had to survive on scraps in the flimsiest of shelters. I became convinced that a planned economy was the only way to use to the maximum the resources of our country, including the brains and skills of men and women. Human beings seemed to me endowed with limitless potentialities, but under capitalism these potentialities are commercialised and directed away from benefiting society, to serve the few."[127] Subsequently *Jessie Street* saw the concept of a state planned economy and *Socialism* according to the political intentions of the *Australian Labor Party* at that time as the preferred social and economic order. "I began to see the Depression as the consequence of the lack of coordination of production, distribution and exchange with the needs and purchasing power of society, and the absence of the controls necessary to protect the rights of all. 'Each man for himself and the devil take the hindmost' seemed to be the premise for this lack of coordination."[128]

Where is the social net in such times? Where are the larger families and the friends helping each other with their abilities to provide goods and services from their private household production in order to substitute the lack of money and purchasing power? The supply of money has become the *ultima ratio* for many private households, in particular those situated in cities where people have to live in blocks of flats. Furthermore, those citizens who cannot take part in the cash economy or even in the *black market* most likely have to face the worst outcome of a depression.

2.2 Private Household Compositions

Now to the central theme of this research monograph - that is the various factors which affect the private households and their money supply as a consequence of reduced private household production and the integration of private household production into the development of an economy.[129] These three subject matters are:

- *Industrialisation of private household production,*
- *Mechanisation of private household production,*
- and *Centralisation of private household production.*

---

[127] Coltheart (2004), p. 80
[128] ibid.
[129] See for specific details Fischer (1982), pp. 69-122

The household composition determines, among other factors, whether the industrialisation, the mechanisation or the centralisation of private household production will proceed in a more encompassing manner in the sense of reducing the various facilities of private household production. When the trend of reduced size of private household increases over the next decades it will enlarge the dependency on money supply to buy and maintain industrial goods and services as well as to acquire private household equipments. This development is for private households in many cases irreversible. In addition, in the sphere of this process, the '*free market*' does not supply anymore those obsolete goods, services and household equipment of an earlier stage of the industrialisation and mechanisation of private household production, once the industries have reached a new technical and organisational level.

Household size and household type determine essentially the equipment of private households with staples as well as their living situation. The results of the *Household Composition and Income and Consumption Sample Survey* 2008 (EVS, *Einkommens- und Verbrauchsstichprobe*) show in Germany in 2008 an unbroken trend to the Single Household. In 2003 the portion of one-person households was 36% and rose to 38% in 2008. Meanwhile from the 39.1 million private households in Germany about 15 million are one-person households. The portion of two-person households remained nearly unchanged with about 34%. In the beginning of 2008 the households with three and more persons made up the remaining 27% of all households. The portion of these multi person households added up to 30% in 2003. The average household size, that is the number of persons on average of all private households, comes in total to 2.1 persons in 2008.[130] It is extraordinary that households with a single person and couples without children add up to 67.1% of all households in Germany in 2008.

When compared with Australia in 2006 for *Lone Person Households as a percentage of all households, based on Place of Usual Residence*,[131] then the results show 24% of all private households are lone households [132] and a similar trend to one person households is revealed, although Australia is an immigration country, which rejuvenates itself by new migrants and their families.

---

[130] Statistisches Bundesamt (German Federal Bureau of Statistics) (2009) Zu Hause in Deutschland, Ausstattung und Wohnsituation privater Haushalte, Wiesbaden

[131] See Appendix 2

[132] Australian Bureau of Statistics (2007) Census 2006, No: 20630-qm29-Australia (Australia)

Structure of Households on 1st of January 2008 according to the Household Composition Income and Consumption Sample Survey 2008, Germany[133]

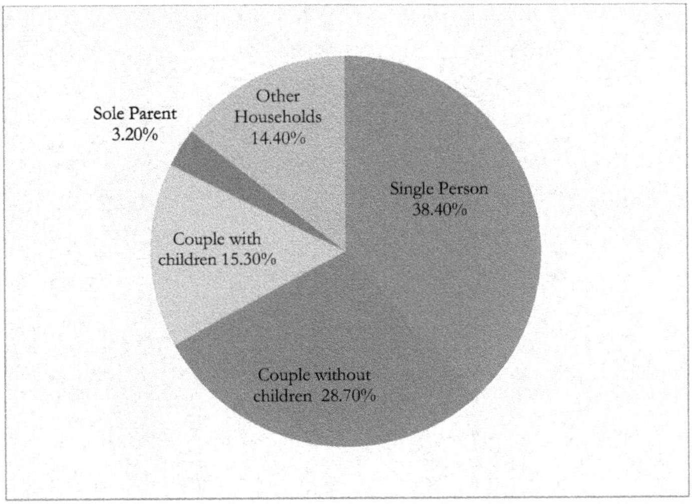

Social Status of the Main Income Earner 1.1.2008, Germany[134]

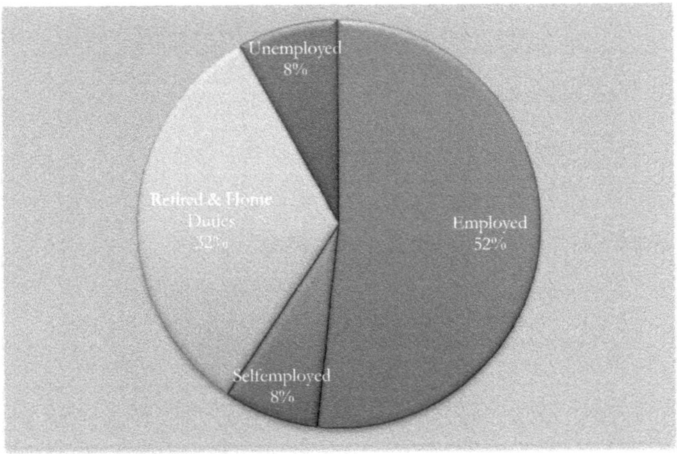

133 Statistisches Bundesamt (German Federal Bureau of Statistics) (2009) Zu Hause in Deutschland, Ausstattung und Wohnsituation privater Haushalte, Wiesbaden

134 ibid.

Lone Person Households, as a percentage of all households, based on place of usual residence, 2006, Australia by States[135]

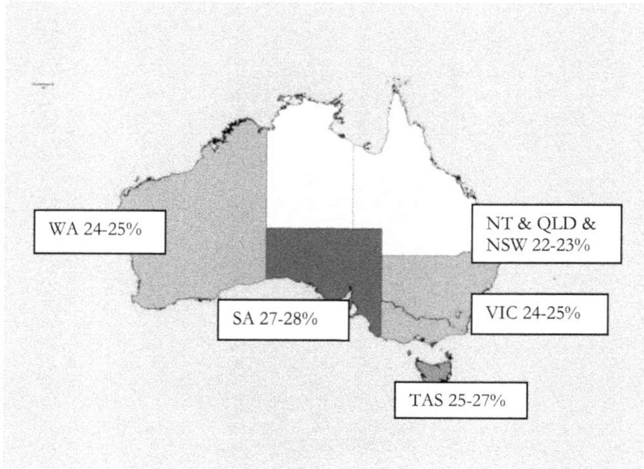

Household Composition, Australia 1996, 2001 and 2006 Census[136] [137]

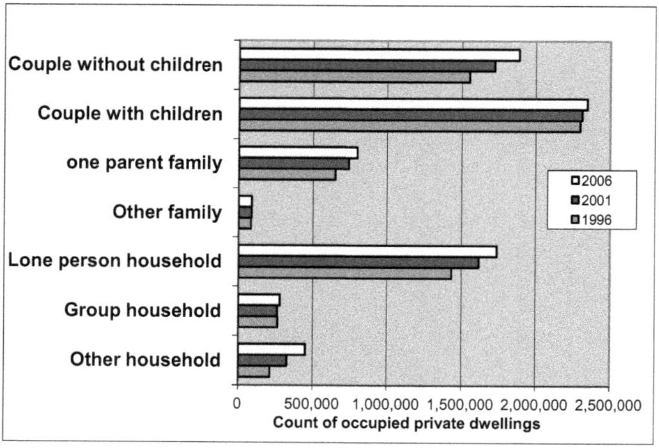

[135] Australian Bureau of Statistics (2007) Census 2006, No: 20630-qm29-Australia, Canberra
[136] Australian Bureau of Statistic (2010) 2006 Census of Population and Housing, Canberra
[137] Explanations see Appendix 5

It is notable that the number of 'Family Households with Children' has dropped in relation to the share of all types of households. Nevertheless the projected number of households, household type 2006 to 2031, Australia, shows that lone person households will grow substantially although in line with family households. Furthermore it has to be taken into account that couple families with no children made up 37% and one parent families 16% in 2006 in Australia.[138]

Household and Family Projections, Australia, 2006 to 2031[139]

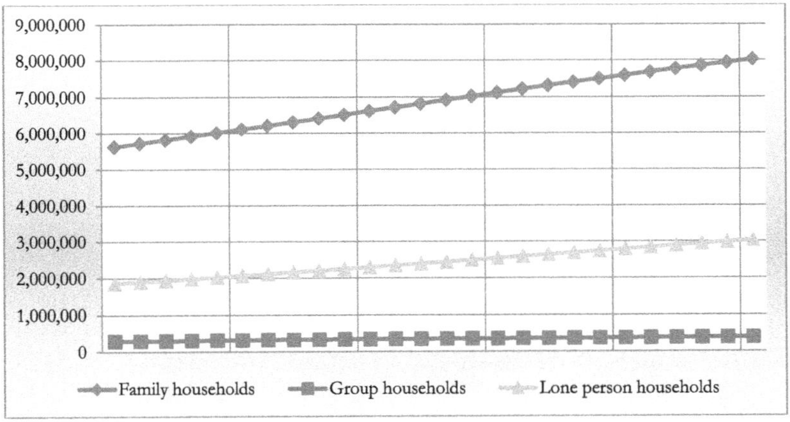

Projected Number of Families, Family Type – 2006 to 2031, Australia, 2006[140]

Couple families with children	Couple families without children	One-parent families	Other families
2,576,014	2,134,939	920,914	103,184
45%	37%	16%	2%

138 ABS 32360DO001_20062031 Household and Family Projections, Australia, 2006 to 2031 Released at 11:30 am (Canberra time) Tues 8 Jun 2010

139 ibid.

140 ibid.

In Western societies, Germany taken as an example, the patterns of consumption are a reflection of the integration of private households into the dependency on markets and of course an indication of the supply of money, which has become an absolute necessity.

Private Households and Expenditure on Consumption of disposable Income per month in 2008, Germany[141]

Expenditure on consumption	Euro	Percentage
Private expenditure on consumption per month	2,245	100.0
Food, beverages, tobacco	321	14.3
Clothes & shoes	106	4.7
Housing, energy, repairs of housing	731	32.6
Interior equipment, household technical goods & equipment	113	5.0
Health care	94	4.2
Transportation	328	14.6
Telecommunications	65	2.9
Leisure, entertainment, culture	255	11.4
Education	20	0.9
Dining out & overnight accommodation	113	5.9
Other goods & services	99	4.4

It seems remarkable that on average private households in Germany have expenditure on food, beverages and tobacco of only 14.3%. Already in the 19th Century the German statistician *Ernst Engel* (1821–1896) made the observation that as income rises, the proportion of income spent on food falls, even if actual expenditure on food rises. *Engel's Law* doesn't imply that food spending remains unchanged as income increases: It suggests that consumers increase their expenditures for food products (in % terms) less than their increases in income.[142]

141 Statistisches Bundesamt (2010), Wo bleibt mein Geld? Ergebnisse der Einkommens- und Verbrauchsstichprobe 2008, Wiesbaden, Germany, p. 23

142 http://en.wikipedia.org/wiki/Engel's_law

Engel's Law[143]

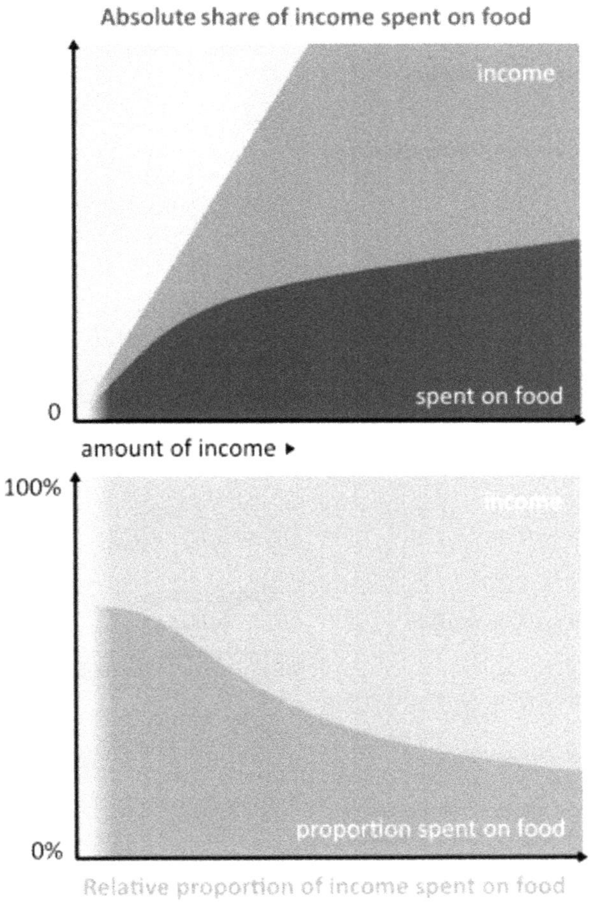

[143] http://upload.wikimedia.org/wikipedia/commons/e/e4/EngelsLaw.svg

Private Households and Expenditure on Consumption of disposable Income per month for selected types of household in 2008, Germany[144]

Expenditure on consumption	Single person		Single parent	
	Euro	%	Euro	%
Private expenditure on consumption per month	1,418	100	1,740	100
Food, beverages, tobacco	182	12.9	281	16.1
Clothes & shoes	58	4.1	94	5.4
Housing, energy, repairs of housing	532	37.5	614	35.3
Interior equipment, household technical goods & equipment	62	4.4	84	4.8
Health care	60	4.3	45	2.6
Transportation	172	12.1	213	12.2
Telecommunications	50	3.5	69	4.0
Leisure, entertainment, culture	161	11.4	174	10.0
Education	6	0.5	28	1.6
Dining out & overnight accommodation	69	4.8	58	3.3
Other goods & services	65	4.6	80	4.6

Expenditure on consumption	Couple without children		Couple with children	
	Euro	%	Euro	%
Private expenditure on consumption per month	2,622	100	3,017	100
Food, beverages, tobacco	360	13.7	478	15.9
Clothes & shoes	115	4.4	167	5.5
Housing, energy, repairs of housing	817	31.2	923	30.6
Interior equipment, household technical goods & equipment	141	5.4	162	5.4
Health care	139	5.3	86	2.9
Transportation	392	15.0	463	15.3
Telecommunications	64	2.4	82	2.7
Leisure, entertainment, culture	315	12.0	335	11.1
Education	11	0.4	52	1.7
Dining out & overnight accommodation	152	5.8	138	4.6
Other goods & services	116	4.4	131	4.3

[144] Statistisches Bundesamt (2010), Wo bleibt mein Geld? Ergebnisse der Einkommens- und Verbrauchsstichprobe 2008, Wiesbaden, Germany, p. 25

However, compared with the expenditure on food, beverage and tobacco with regard to different types of private households, the single parent household spends 16.1% more than all other households and less with only 3.3% spending on dining out and overnight accommodation.

Sometimes the relatively small proportion of expenditure in particular on food is taken as a sign of a developed 'wealthy' country (e.g. Germany), which obviously enables the average private household to spend far more on other goods and services, for example on leisure, entertainment, and culture as well as on housing, energy, and repairs of housing. Nevertheless, the *food security* of a country might be in doubt if a downfall in the economy through various reasons (e.g. war, natural disaster, worldwide depression) occurs. Without factual evidence one might hypothetically argue where are the 'reserves' for food production to maintain a reasonable supply of food? In cities in Germany after World War II private households had, among other measures, access to allotments to grow their own vegetables at least. But this seems to be not so much in fashion anymore since the supply of food through the supermarket chains are provided and people are trusting that this state of affairs will last. On the other hand it has to be taken into account that the economic condition of the so called 'average' private household is just a statistical indicator, but in reality in many civilized Western countries the income distribution among the entire private households is by no means near to be equal. "As we look over the country today we see two classes of people. The excessively rich and the abject poor, and between them is a gulf ever deepening, ever widening, and the ranks of the poor are continually being recruited from a third class, the well-to-do, which class is rapidly disappearing and being absorbed by the very poor."[145] Drastically compared to the 19th Century one might conjecture whether in general only few conditions have changed?

2.3 Equipment of Households with Household Appliances

In all sections of private household production[146]

- Planning of the sections of private household production
- Nutrition
- Internal transport

---

145 Milford Wriarson Howard (1862-1937) The American Plutocracy (1895), in: Reinert, Erik S. (2013) Civilizing capitalism: "good" and "bad" greed from the enlightenment to Thorstein Veblen (1857-1929), in: real-world economics review, issue no. 63, p. 57

146 Fischer (1982), pp. 42-43

- Storage
- Shopping
- Household cleaning
- Clothing
- Gardening and domestic animal care
- Personal care of household members

the equipment of private households with household appliances has widely occurred among the private households and in addition steadily improved since the beginning of the 20th Century. The production of, for instance, fridges, electrical and gas operated stoves, as well as washing machines was initially a matter for large kitchens and laundries in for example hospitals, restaurants, hotels and canteens for industrial workers or for military accommodation. With some technical innovations provided to the household appliances industry, the production of smaller appliances could support the increased demand and supply. People who could afford to buy such household appliances were mostly driven by the substitution of hard and exhaustive female work in the private household production. Later on the household appliances industry developed more and more refined and sometimes sophisticated technical goods once the market for simple appliances was saturated. In particular since the 1960s market research and marketing facilitated or even formed the demand for a wide range of technical goods for private households. In modern times for instance the equipping of private households with information technology products like home computers and mobile phones has increased substantially. One of several effects was the establishment of online shopping, which became an alternative within the household production section of shopping. People were able to abandon the traditional way of buying in shops and supermarkets as well as in shopping centres, and then people were saved from transporting various goods to their place of residence.

The following graphs illustrate the relative saturation of technical goods:[147][148]

---

[147] Statistisches Bundesamt (2008) Wirtschaftsrechnungen, Einkommens- und Verbrauchsstichprobe 2008, Ausstattung privater Haushalte mit ausgewählten Gebrauchsgütern, Fachserie 15, Heft 1, Wiesbaden

[148] See Appendix 3 for more details

Equipment of private households with staples in Germany 1998, 2003 & 2008

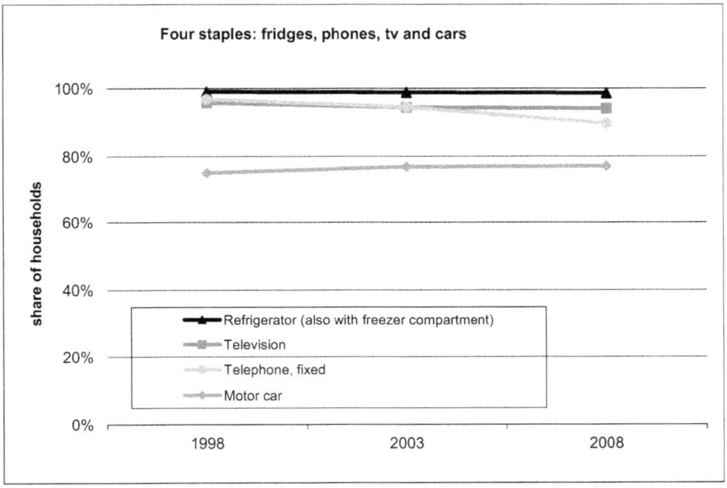

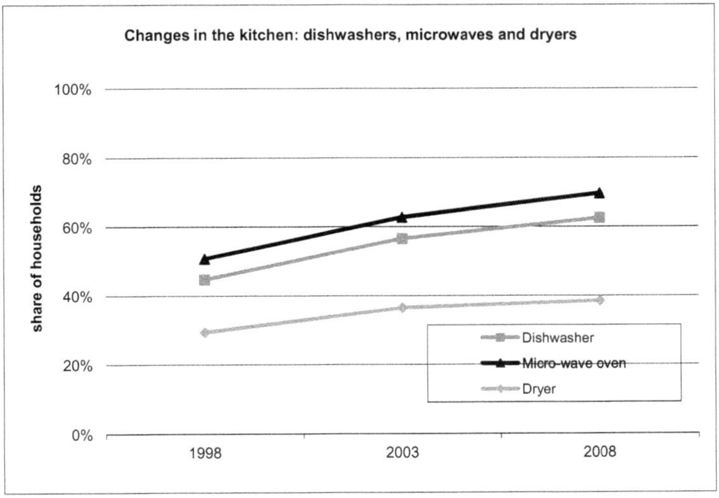

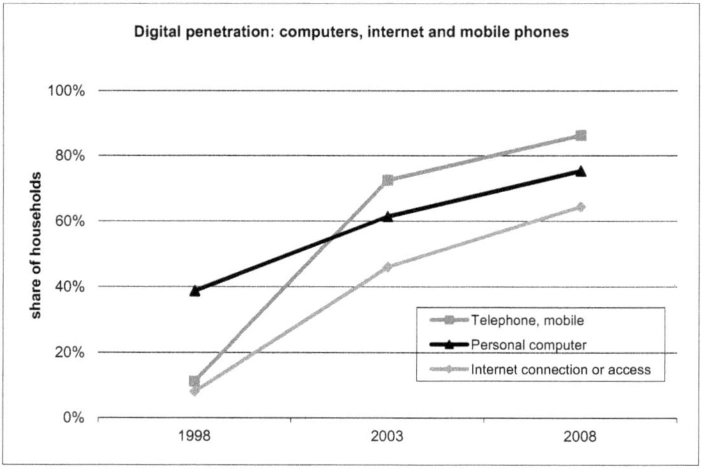

The equipment of private households with staples shows unmistakably the progress of the mechanization of the private household production and the substantial loss of private household production within the households in comparison to former times around the beginning of the 20th Century.

2.4 Market Power of Service and Retail Companies

The market power of *service and retail companies* is capable of shaping the process of the *industrialisation, mechanisation and centralisation of private household production.* In particular if the degree of concentration of market power, especially in the grocery section, is highly concentrated in a few companies with a large number of outlets all over a country. This is the case in Australia, where two companies Woolworth and Coles determine what supply is offered to private households. Recently the supply has gone to mostly so called 'cheap' products imported from Asia including China. In addition the Australian hardware and clothing stores, including the 'daughters' of the two dominant grocery suppliers Big-W, Target and K-Mart, provide mostly Chinese products and clothing. Some shopping centres appear as 'Chinese warehouses'. However, one should bear in mind that Australian consumers were willing to buy those products and subsequently supported the decrease in a wide range of the Australian manufacturing industries. Furthermore the Federal Australian Governments contributed substantially to such retrogression through their ongoing policy of lowering the tariffs and their policies to rely on the world market in many ways.[149]

Shimshon Bichler and *Jonathan Nitzan* strongly assert in their new cosmology of capitalism that capital has to be seen also as a sign of power. "It argues that capital is not a narrow economic entity, but a symbolic quantification of power. Capital is not absolute, it is relative. It has little to do with utility or abstract labor, and it extends far beyond machines and production lines. Most broadly, it represents the organized power of dominant capital groups to create the order of their society."[150] One example may be the current *Hypermarkets,* which are superstores combining supermarkets and department stores.[151]

"The result is an expansive retail facility carrying a wide range of products under one roof, including full groceries lines and general merchandise. In theory, *hypermarkets* allow customers to satisfy all their routine shopping needs in one trip".[152]

The produce section of a typical Wal-Mart Supercenter (Wal-Mart's hypermarket brand)[153]

---

149 Fischer & Byron (1995); see also "Ausbuy" in Wikipedia: http://en.wikipedia.org/wiki/Ausbuy
150 Bichler & Nitzan (2012)
151 See also Appendix 1
152 http://en.wikipedia.org/wiki/Hypermarket
153 ibid.

In past decades in Australia and most OECD-Countries the retail sector has undergone a significant concentration of ownership in retail trading. A few very large and dominant supermarket chains, franchise companies and shopping centres has lead to a trading philosophy of *'Anytime, everywhere, everything the same'*. This trading philosophy characterised by the author, which means that large supermarkets as well as warehouses have centrally driven procurement policies; they demand bulk orders from specific price competitive producers and farmers, nor do these retail giants acknowledge special local features.[154] The result is a monotonous shopping atmosphere at these venues. For example in Australia there are numerous franchise business shops with cheap and often low-quality products from China and elsewhere. The public activities of several campaigns to *'Buy Australian Made'* had little impact on consumers' purchasing decisions in times when household budgets were getting tighter.[155]

Furthermore there has been a loss of regional flair, which was in former times attained through preservation of regionally distinctive features and peculiarities. However, regional markets with locally operated shops have almost disappeared. Usually these are small businesses with predominantly family ownership. This is consistent with changes in other countries where the range of goods on offer and the structure of business have changed dramatically. For example in *Germany* the supermarkets on the outskirts of towns have diluted the supply and, as well, the demand in the central business district. After the introduction of the *Euro* on 1 January 2002 a renewed shift in buyer behaviour occurred. The big department stores have noticed a reduction in sales and discount food chains, which now stock all consumer goods right up to computers, have indicated a clear shift in sales. The cause is the uncertainness of the consumer. The inexplicable price increase due to the monetary change, the shortage of money because of the recession in Germany and the willingness of brand name manufacturers to allow discount chains to sell their goods, has brought about a change in old habits. The monotony of the self-service stores with the sale out of cardboard boxes, without a hint of service, has taken hold.[156]

Street markets have been rediscovered by stallholders and consumers as a countervailing power to regain regional markets with a closer relationship between producers and consumers. Even Local Governments have started to promote these markets not only as an opportunity to revitalise the city life but also as a tourist attraction. One might argue that street markets are an ideal place for tax evasion,

---

[154] Fischer (2004), p. ix
[155] Fischer & Byron (1995)
[156] Krausbeck (2002), p. 21

and therefore they should be strongly policed by the tax office. Often this accusation is based on a hidden agenda, which is the extinction of these growing markets. The informal markets offer value for money for consumers and in addition require little capital investment for stallholders to participate in the lucrative business at the expense of the established retail shops.

The role of small businesses as the backbone of the economy has been threatened in the Australian retail industry by the emergence of the supermarket giants. This agglomeration has been accompanied by these giants exercising their market power both as buyers and sellers in an ever-expanding range of retail services. This has had important implications for small businesses, particularly the resulting willingness of these small businesses to adapt to these changes and in order to survive, to participate in the informal retail sector that comprises the weekend, night and street markets. As buyers, the retail giants are able to affect prices paid to producers with the result that small producers are forced to leave the industry, or seek other markets.

A good example of this in Australia has been the removal of price controls in the fresh milk industry, and the loss of the small independent milk producers, who either left the industry or found alternative markets. One such market was the informal market, the street markets. Here the small producers are able to sell their produce direct to the public as value added products such as cheese or butter, even though this may be a less efficient method from the producer's point of view; it may be the last opportunity for the producer to stay in the industry. As sellers, the retail giants have moved beyond a virtual duopoly as sellers, to a situation where they have become brands in themselves. This puts them in direct competition with the major brand names in retail. Not only do the supermarket giants now have the ability to collude to manipulate prices, but they also have the power of product control in the market place. If this was not of sufficient concern, the area of activity of these giants is expanding to include fresh produce, petrol, alcohol, insurance and banking. Here the smaller retailers are being squeezed out of their businesses and in an attempt to survive, are forced into the informal market as vendors, initially to clear their stocks, and then as the only means available to remaining retailers.

Some are finding unexpected support from the larger manufacturers of *'brand name'* products who are dissatisfied with their own treatment at the hands of the retail giants.[157] 'The supermarkets hope to boost their profit margins by stocking more private-label brands. Manufacturers stand to gain as well. In the food sector in

---

[157] Fleming (2002), pp. 14-15

particular, most manufacturers in Australia are operating with spare capacity and are keen to win tenders to produce private-label groceries for the biggest retailers, Coles Supermarkets, Woolworths Supermarkets and Metcash".[158] *John Liefeld* condensed the matter to the basic predicament in the retail industry: "The real issue is the centralization of control of the market for consumer packaged goods in the hands of a small number of massive chains and multinationals. In Canada, as centralization, through mergers in the retailing industries, food, general merchandise and hardware and home maintenance, is resulting in a situation of monopolistic/oligopoly (to coin a new category), sectors of the economy which typically had been characterized by more competitive situations".[159]

The *Australian Bureau of Statistics (ABS)* defines the Retail Trade Industry in the Retail Census 1998-99 as "businesses mainly engaged in the resale of new or used goods to final consumers for personal or household consumption, or in selected repair activities such as repair of household equipment or motor vehicles".[160] Australian national market share figures are supplied by the industry publication *Retail World*, which made use of information drawn from the ACNielsen Research of 5000 households.

Retail Trade Market Share[161]

	April 2002	April 2003
Woolworths/ Safeway	34.0%	35.5%
Coles/Bi-Lo	32.5%	33.7%
Franklins (NSW)	5.8%	2.2%
Action (WA, QLD)	1.5%	2.3%
Aldi (NSW, VIC)	0.8%	1.2%
Others	25.4%	25.1%

Since the establishment of *supermarkets* in Western economies after *WWII*, there has been a significant evolution; manufacturers and consumers became gradually more distant from one another with limited or no personal connection at all, for instance with regard to the establishment of large transnationals and national

158 Lloyd (2005)
159 Liefeld (2005)
160 ABS (2000) Catalogue No. 8622.0, 2
161 Safe (2003), p. 26

companies like in Australia where the whole sector is primarily controlled by two or three major companies. The separation of producers and consumers is often attributed to the industrial revolution. What has changed since the war is the balance of power in the distribution channel from manufacturer to retailer. This is sometimes argued as a good thing because 'retailers are closer to consumers'. However, *Robert Lawson* believes a substantial danger is that retailers have short-term perspectives – especially with the low inventories they carry. They are a long way from the supply side issues that face farmers etc where long-term investments are necessary or environmental protection becomes a problem.

The rapid development of technology made it impossible for consumers to examine sufficiently products and services due to a lack of knowledge. In particular after WWII *'planned obsolescence'* forced consumers to purchase deliberately inferior products to keep the industry engaged. New marketing strategies including sophisticated advertising were developed to convince consumers of their so-called 'needs', creating a business environment in which sometimes misleading and fraudulent business practices disadvantaged individual consumers.

For example: "At Toys 'R' US on New York's Time Square an animated black and green dinosaur looms over milling crowds, occasionally growling and swivelling its head. Wandering magicians conjure tricks for customers and store managers with pockets full of tiny toys move in quickly to calm anxious toddlers. There is a pervading sense of fun, of being in a magical world of entertainment, of enchantment. It is of course all craftily designed to entice customers to buy more toys".[162]

A more detailed picture of the retail trade industry might be drawn from the Retail Census 1998-99 *(Australian Bureau of Statistics, October 2000)*. In 1998–99 the supermarkets and grocery stores industry generated the highest income ($38.8 billion) which was 23 per cent of the total income for the retail trade industry. This was followed by motor vehicle services, which generated $25.2 billion in income, or 15 per cent of total income.[163]

162 Wood (2004), p.7
163 ABS (2002) Catalogue No. 8622.0, 10

Industry Group Contribution to Retail Income[164]

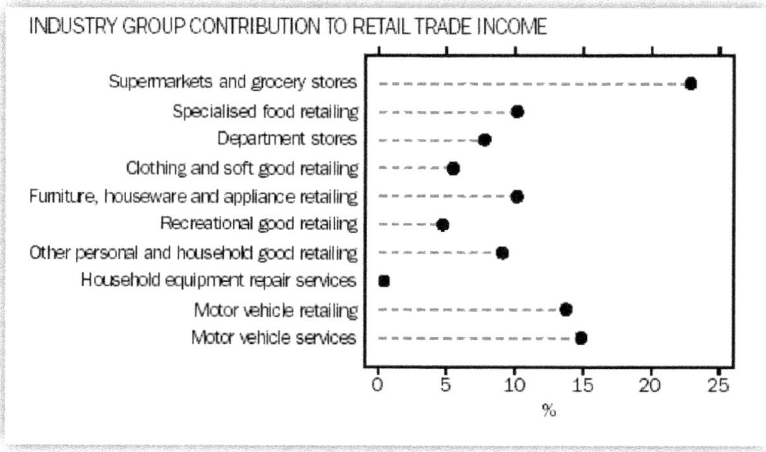

2.5 Consumer Associations

The development of the private household production through the *industrialization,* the *mechanisation* and the *centralisation* is also dependent on the market power private households are able to exercise. If, for instance, a minority of private households insists on buying good quality products and services but the majority has switched to much cheaper suppliers, then most likely if certain goods and services are not profitable to produce or to sell within the retail sector these products and services disappear over time. As an example may be given that in former times many households were sewing their own clothes with a sewing machine and with a variety of seams and patterns. However, within decades after *WWII* the textile industry has nearly completely taken over this section of the private household production. Furthermore, which private household is able to repair their shoes or even can deliver them for repair to a shoemaker –shoes in the sense of a throw away article are in fashion today. With the retrogression of private household production, then the information of consumers becomes more and more essential. The private households are dependent on the market and the involved marketing activities.

In particular, the consumer's right to information indicates a failure in the provision of proper market information to consumers. This is not only related to

164 ABS (2002) Catalogue No. 8622.0, 10

consumer goods and services but also to services provided, for instance by financial institutions, espousing the consumer's right to receive proper, clearly understandable information even about 'invisible' products like credit. It might be argued that legislation is necessary to enforce standards of market behaviour, and the existence of effective legislation and consumer protection authorities creates an awareness of the rights of consumers throughout the community".[165]

Swan has asserted that "to suggest that the consumer can be fully protected by regulations during a continual process of evolutionary change is of course complete nonsense". [166] Nevertheless, this might lead to questions about the costs of regulation rather than to the principal issue of social obligations to consumers who failed in managing their private consumption properly.

Given the facts of the development and performance of consumer information, and taking into account the ultimate need for consumer protection, then the provision of consumer protection through legislation is currently based on the idea that the individual might ultimately seek resolution through court action.

However: "Access to the courts is based on the same egalitarian principles as access to the London Ritz - open to the rich and poor alike. In reality, it is a privilege few can afford. Research in the UK by the *Office of Fair Trading* (Annual Report, 1991) has revealed that only a tiny proportion of consumers with complaints pursue these as far as to a court or another dispute resolution procedure".[167] In 1996 the *European Commission of the European Communities* has issued an Action Plan on consumer access to justice and the settlement of consumer disputes in the internal market. On condition that consumers made a complaint to a company and tried to solve their problems, it does not necessarily mean that the actions taken were forced by court orders.

The *United Nations* has proclaimed March 15 as *World Consumer Rights Day* and has set up Guidelines for Consumer Protection. Among the eight international consumer rights the right to redress requires measures enabling consumers to obtain redress:

- Governments should establish or maintain legal and or administrative measures to enable consumers or, as appropriate, relevant organisations to obtain redress through formal or informal procedures that are expeditious, fair, inexpensive

---

[165] Goldring (1987), p. 4
[166] Swan (1987), p. 12
[167] Gibson (1992), p. 407

and accessible. Such procedures should take particular account of the needs of lower income consumers.

- Governments should encourage all enterprises to resolve consumer disputes in a fair, expeditious and informal manner, and to establish voluntary mechanisms, including advisory services and informal complaints procedures, which can provide assistance to consumers.
- Information on available redress and other dispute resolving procedures should be made available to consumers.[168]

In its Action Plan 1996 on consumer access to justice and the settlement of consumer disputes in the internal market the European Commission set up a Working Outline for a Recommendation Establishing Criteria for the Creation of Out-of-Court Procedures Applicable to Consumer Disputes in the Member States. The way this question is answered also determines the magnitude of the gap between the theoretical construct designed by the legislator and voters' day-to-day lives: it is the small disputes of everyday life that give ordinary consumers an opportunity to gauge the effectiveness of the law - and not the headline-making court cases, which rarely concern them.

Since the 1980s consumers are showing a change in their behaviour within *OECD* countries. Increasingly, consumers are concerned by production methods, together with preoccupations about the environment, conditions surrounding production in certain less-developed countries, or the welfare of animals and a particular concern is food consumption; the concern about *Bovine spongiform encephalopathy*, commonly known as mad cow disease, chemical residues, genetic modifications, irradiation of food, all contribute to a general unease about food quality and relevant controls and responsibilities. In a market economy, the main responsibility for environmental degradation thus lies with the consumer. Realistically, however, ordinary consumers have little knowledge of the links between consumption patterns and their consequences, and have little real power to affect the market place. In a highly industrialised society, knowledge and responsibility are so diffused among economic actors that no one really feels responsible.[169] Finally it has to be noted that: Currently, one fifth of the world's population, i.e. Western consumers, use four fifths of the world's resources.[170]

[168] Healey (1995), p. 8
[169] Heiskanen & Pantzar (1997), p. 409
[170] ibid., p. 413

A further area of consumer affairs is the meanwhile widespread consumer credit, either as unsecured personal loans, overdraft facilities or credit card debts. Within the *OECD* countries it is seen as common sense that consumer affairs authorities and consumer organizations play an important role in supplementing educational efforts to make students aware about the credit industry and of the financial and legal aspects involved with different kinds of consumer credit. In most *OECD* countries *consumer affairs* is not a compulsory and independent subject in the curriculum of post primary schools, but often a part of home economics, law and business studies, and partially in economics. *Consumer education* should commence in high school at the latest, and should be provided in tertiary, as well as in technical and further education courses. One aim could be the provision of advice on a loan if consumers are willing to get a second and independent opinion before they sign the contract. This work might be done by official and non-profit agencies like for instance *Consumer Information Centres* (Verbraucherzentralen) in Germany, assuming there are relevant funds for operation available for ongoing periods. It would further be facilitated through minimum requirements of disclosures for consumer credit contracts and standardized methods for determining the effective annual interest rate as a subject of Consumer Credit Legislation.

Traditionally bad debts were seen as losses which financial institutions bore as a part of their business, with share holders initially bearing the burden. It is now the case that the costs of bad debts are passed by cross-subsidy within the system of a financial institution to other consumers, even to those who have no loans and simply pay a fee for operating a savings account. This practice has to be abolished. The preferred method to do so is the adoption, by all financial organizations, of the calculation of interest rates based on the individual consumers' credit risk, rather than the imposition of a blanket rate. For low income consumers or beneficiaries who are the most vulnerable for consumer credit insurance, consideration should be given to whether the premium might be refunded to the consumer totally or partially by a government funding scheme, as a step forward in social policy to avoid a financial breakdown and hardship of these affected groups.

Consumer education should focus on the study of the marketplace. This includes the study of consumers, their decision processes and behaviours, the analysis of markets and their structure, and the interactions among and between consumers & buyers & clients and producers & providers of goods and services, government and regulatory processes. Basically consumers learn in several fundamental ways, e.g. four elements seem to be significant: motive, cue, response and reinforcement. The exact nature and strength of these components influence what will be learned, how well it will be learned and the rate at which learning will occur.[171]

- Motives arouse individuals, thereby increasing their readiness to respond.
- A cue may be viewed as a stimulus not strong enough to arouse consumers, but capable of providing direction to motivated activity.
- A response may be viewed as a mental or physical activity the consumer makes in reaction to a stimulus situation. Responses appropriate to a particular situation are learned over time through experience in facing that situation.
- Reinforcement is anything that follows a response and increases the tendency for the response to recur in a similar situation.[172]

In a non-representative survey *Questionnaire Private Household*[173], undertaken in late January 2013 til early February 2013 a questionnaire was sent by the author as a web link provided by *SurveyMonkey*[174] [175] and via email, randomly distributed to roughly 1,000 interviewees. The third question was "Should domestic science be a compulsory subject in primary schools for a period of more than two years?" The response rate came up to 7.7% with non-representative results.

Astonishingly an overwhelmingly majority of 75.3% of respondents[176] agreed that *domestic science* should be a compulsory subject in primary schools for a period of more than two years. Obviously people realise that the knowledge to manage a private household for instance from nutrition to care of sickness is lacking substantially. In previous years *domestic science* was regarded as being relevant for female pupils exclusively, then later on male pupils were included, but the ministries of education in most developed countries regarded domestic science only as relevant for the so called 'lower' educated pupils. This subject was classified more and more as historically obsolete and the natural sciences were preferred. Nevertheless, the common knowledge for performing private household production faded since WWII at least and is irreversibly lost for the generations to come.

---

171 Lawson (1996), p. 392

172 ibid.

173 See Appendix 4 Questionnaire Private Household

174 SurveyMonkey is a web survey development cloud based (SaaS) company, founded in 1999 by Ryan Finley. The company acquired as a private limited until 2009, where it was sold to a private equity consortium. In 2010, the company received US$100 million in debt financing from Bank of America Merrill Lynch, and SunTrust Robinson Humphrey. SurveyMonkey has 185 employees, with offices in Palo Alto, California, Portland, Oregon, Seattle, Washington, Lisbon, São Paulo, and Luxembourg. It claims over 12 million registered customers.
See also: http://en.wikipedia.org/wiki/SurveyMonkey

175 BASIC account: the limits of a BASIC account are 100 responses free.

176 See age composition of respondents in chapter 5.1

Q3. Should domestic science be a compulsory subject in primary schools for a period of more than two years?[177]

	Response Percent	Response Count
Yes	75.3%	58
No	18.2%	14
N/A	6.5%	5
	answered question	77
	skipped question	0

Moreover, the United Nations insist that consumer education should pay special attention to the needs of disadvantaged consumers in both urban and rural areas.[178] Therefore *Larsen* suggests the improvement in the following areas:

- Awareness and understanding of consumer rights.
- Awareness and understanding of consumer organisations and consumer legislation.
- Gathering and use of consumer and product/service information.
- Complaint behaviour.
- Business education.[179]

2.6 Government Intervention and Private Household Production

Referring to the central theme of the nature and development of private household production the question arises whether in times like in Australia today the private households have the opportunity to fall into a *safety net* or are covered by a *buffer zone* to cope with an economy in recession at the least or even sliding into a depression? For many private households there are most likely none and they have to adjust to the circumstances of reducing their expenditure while feeling the pinch of an economic downfall. There are a variety of *Government interventions* like, for example, the fiscal policy from tax policy to easing money policy and monetary policy

177 See also Appendix 4
178 Larsen (1998), p. 30
179 ibid., p. 151

through interest rate variations. Each of these policies has an impact on the sections of private household production.

The situation gets even worse when a country like Australia has lost its capacity and ability to maintain sufficient manufacturing industries.[180] The consequence is then to rely on imports from the world market, in particular from China. Sometimes like in Australia the Government sponsors a *moral suasion* about an appeal to the consumers to buy products and services that are Australian made and even provided by Australian owned companies.[181]

The *'Buy Australian Made'* Campaign is an example of a moral suasion argument which urges consumers to buy consumer goods made in their own country to reduce high import penetration, unemployment and the current, enormous trade deficit of the Australian economy. Studies of the 'Buy Australian Made' Campaign have been either enthusiastic[182] or harsh attacks upon the 'Buy Australian Made' Campaign. [183]

Obviously there is a strong correlation between the decrease of tariffs since the 1970s and the increase of *import penetration.* To lower tariffs for a whole variety of consumer goods is part of the so called 'Microeconomic Reform' process. Further one has to bear in mind that fights between supporters of free trade and protectionism for the benefit of the country's economy have existed already in the colonies of Australia in the 19th century.

Various country of origin campaigns, e.g. *Shop Canadian - Made in Canada*, *Buy American* or *Buy German Produce*, are basically intended to convince the consumers of the idea that domestic products are synonymous with high quality, regardless of whether this is in fact the case.

The *'Australian Made'* logo, provided by the *Advance Australia Foundation*, is the official Federal Government symbol. A licence to carry the logo can be granted for a product for which at least more than 50 percent of the factory or work cost occurred in Australia, or at least 50 percent of costs occurred in Australia but granting of such a licence with respect to that product is deemed to have significant benefit to the Australian economy or be of significant public advantage. However, granting a licence does not necessarily mean that the product possesses high performance characteristics or is of high quality.

---

[180] See Appendix 6 with regard to the dominant commodities exports and manufactured imports
[181] Gallagher (2007), p.25-29
[182] Marsden Jacob Associates (1994)
[183] Black (1995)

Over the last decades numerous empirical studies about the relationship between price and quality in consumer markets have been undertaken, and the overall result is that the statistical relationship is rather weak. Consumers use price as a quality indicator if the price is the only source of information. Therefore consumers need more information about quality performance. The *country of origin* of goods, taken as a quality indicator, may perhaps influence consumer's choice of goods and the price they are willing to pay.

Data from the 1991-92 Retail and Services Census (ABS) outline the dominance by supermarkets and grocery stores of the Australian retail sector, and it is an important matter which buying policies these stores adopt in relation to imported goods, or in other words, what consumer goods are available on the shelves. The data might be 'old' but the situation has changed towards a higher concentration of the two large supermarket and grocery companies in the Australian market.

The benefits of labelling country of origin via regulation could be justified if the information for consumers essentially affects their purchase decision. Therefore a consumer survey and a retailer survey have been undertaken in 1994 by the author and *Peter Byron*.[184]

The *consumer survey* involved surveying 647 consumers in the Townsville area of North Queensland, Australia, in order to determine the importance they placed upon a product's country of manufacture. A certain degree of caution must be exercised with the findings of the consumer survey as only two example products were used (male business shirts and packets of tea bags) to determine the respondent's reactions to country of manufacture information. If a different range of products had been used some aspects of the findings reported here may have been significantly different.

Respondents in the consumer survey indicated that price, quality and value for money were the over-riding factors in their buying decision process in relation to the displayed products. While a majority of respondents indicated that they viewed country of manufacture as being important they were much more likely to select the Australian product if the Australian product represented good value for money. Younger respondents, i.e. less than 30 years old, regarded country of manufacture as being less important than older respondents. In relation to shirts the higher the educational attainment of the respondent the less important the country of

[184] Fischer & Byron (1995), p. 65-160

manufacture was rated and respondents born overseas regarded it as less important than respondents born in Australia.

I Feel that Buying Australian-made Products is Beneficial to the Australian Economy[185]

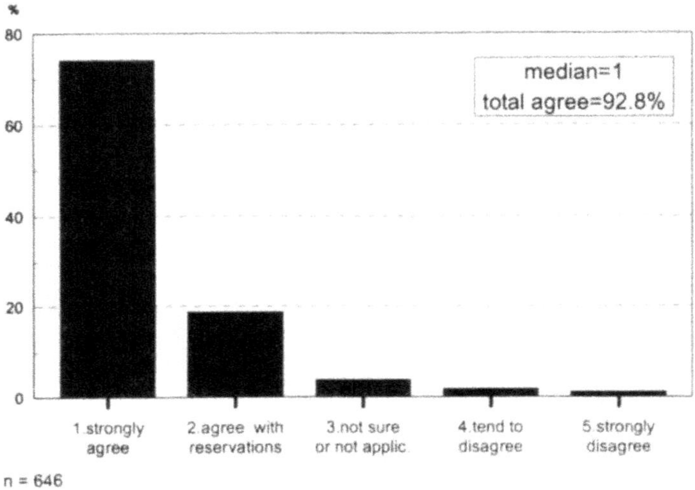

There was overwhelming agreement, 92.8 percent, with the statement that buying Australian-made products benefits the Australian economy. This highlighted a contrast between consumers' intentions and their actions. That is, with the very high level of agreement to this question it would be expected that the respondents would have a strong propensity to buy Australian-made products. However when respondents were confronted earlier on in the survey with the problem of choosing between an Australian-made shirt and an imported shirt, which were identical in every way except for labelling, only 47.2 percent of the respondents chose the Australian shirt.[186]

There was also very strong agreement, 71.1 percent, with the statement that the Federal Government should increase tariffs on imported products in order to make Australian-made goods more competitive. Demographic characteristics showed that female respondents were more in favour of higher tariffs than males but the higher

185 Fischer & Byron (1995), p. 128
186 ibid., p. 129

a respondent's educational qualification the less likely the respondent was to be in favour of higher tariffs. This is perhaps the most surprising of the findings of the survey given the very bad press tariffs have received both in this country and world-wide and the tariff policies of both the major political parties in Australia. It would seem that respondents see a clear relationship between cheaper imported products and domestic employment opportunities and are indicating that they are prepared (to an undetermined extent) to forego the personal benefits of lower prices in exchange for national employment growth.

Michael M Gallagher summed it up in his overall prediction: "In arriving at this 'happy state' the most important thing is to convince the Australian public to look beyond their hip pocket and realise that what they do can determine the future of Australia. This is not the time for feel good gestures by politicians in response to media led pressure. The future of the world is not well served by Australians continuing to enjoy a consumer lead boom financed by money borrowed against future mining only to face long term decline. To change this requires a change of attitude by Australians and Ausbuy is working towards this end."[187]

There are a number of areas that suggested themselves for further possible research. Firstly the buying processes adopted by the major retail chains should be investigated as no information on this area was gained from this survey. It was found that the people running the major supermarket and retail chains in the Townsville area had no input into which products they were to stock. Buying decisions for their operation were made in various head offices and state headquarters around the country. Associated with such additional research could be an investigation of the growth in importance of home brands and whether this is directly influencing the level of import penetration of the Australian market.

But overall, a consumer's responsibility is limited to think primarily of price, quality, durability, availability, time, environment, after sale service, and making a purchasing decision for their own benefit within these parameters. Consumers as individuals should not have an obligation to recognize within their purchasing decisions, what effect this will have for the national economy in the sense of a preferred demand for domestic products. Furthermore, in remote areas, this creates a dilemma through relevant products and services not being available at the right time and at the right location.

---

[187] Gallagher (2007), p. 29

All in all, for a successful 'Buy Australian Made' Campaign there must be a common agreement about an Australian Identity among the people of Australia. But Australia is a large country, a continent with long distances between cities and huge remote areas and it might be that, for instance, consumers in Western Australia are not including in their purchasing behaviour the thought of replacing imports to create jobs for Queenslanders. It is also a risk that with increasing nationalism, those consumers who are buying Australian-made products may be identified as 'Better Aussies' following the motto 'Think Australian-Buy Australian-Be Australian'. An early example of this occurred when the Australian Prime Minister, Mr *Bob Hawke*, launched the *'Australian Made'* Campaign on Sunday, 31 August 1986. He said that 'the campaign is designed to shift consumers' preferences towards Australian products, by giving consumers a sense of national pride and purpose in choosing Australian products over foreign competition.[188]

It seems that consumers are sometimes rediscovered as sovereigns in the sense of *Adam Smith's* consumer sovereignty, but only if the economy has slumped. In early 1995 the Consumer Information Centre, State of Bremen/Germany (North), closed down due to a lack of public funding and one of the first things to be axed as a result of the enormous state budget deficit was the government regulated Consumer Affairs Bureaux. But what about consumerism and those consumer advocates who were fighting for more consumer protection and education in those times when the economy was in good shape?

In countries experiencing economic decline, especially those with a high unemployment level and trade deficit, consumers are urged to buy products made in their own country to help create jobs, assist in defeating unemployment and to avoid import penetration. Sometimes it is a so called 'war against unemployment' where policy makers like to raise an appeal to patriotic behaviour, shifting the responsibility of employment and the level of high import penetration towards consumers.[189] This appeal of moral suasion might often be useful in politics, particularly during an election campaign, but it can also easily lead to a simplification of the economic circumstances of the country.

Relevant examples regarding moral suasion could be some of the campaigns in East-Germany, after the first year of reunification. No doubt, when the West-German Mark was introduced in 1990 to the East-German market, there was a tremendous flow of products made in West-Germany, EC-Countries, Japan and the

---

188 Hawke (1986)
189 Australia Consumers' Association (1993)

USA to the East-German market, because there were few equivalent products available to these consumers for more than four decades. After the reunification, unemployment in all regions of East-Germany increased sharply, the collapse of the previous system was evident and the market became overcrowded with so called western products. Politicians then urged East-Germans to buy East-German-made products, but there was only a small range of products available which were able to reduce this 'import' penetration, in particular those which were formerly exports to western countries to obtain urgently needed western currencies. Some politicians at that time were unable to accept the clear statement that the East-German economy was literally bankrupt.

Fights between supporters of free trade and protectionism existed in the colonies of Australia in the 19th century. Neither the bourgeois parties like the *Liberals* nor the *Trade Unions*, were committed to the political aim of free trade or protectionism. One must bear in mind that traditionally, trade unionism was an instrument for improving the standard of living of the workers within a capitalist society.[190]

But, by the end of 1893, the right of non-unionists to join the Political Labour League was recognised in all colonies and faction fights between free traders and protectionists were widespread. With respect to the bourgeois parties in the colonies of *New South Wales* and *Victoria*, the parties were considerably divided into free traders and protectionists by faction fights in 1891. Nevertheless, both factions were committed to material well-being for all, equality of opportunity, and the career open to talent.[191] These faction fights have to be seen against the background of the federation movement, that is, to abolish trade barriers among the colonies, and to overseas trade to the UK, and among other countries. For example, in the 19th century, the colonial parliaments imposed customs duties on the goods of other colonies, or discriminated against them with differential rail rates.[192]

In the 1970s *Globalisation* became the all embracing idea. *John Ralston Saul* affirmed "Globalization emerged in the 1970s as if from nowhere, fully grown, enrobed in an aura of inclusivity. Advocates and believers argued with audacity that, through the prism of a particular school of economics, societies around the world would be taken in new, interwoven and positive directions. This mission was converted into policy and law over twenty years - the 1980s and '90s - with the force

190 Clark (1992), p. 162
191 ibid., p. 158
192 ibid., p. 162

of declared inevitability."[193] Human activities from politics to social policy and culture were perceived principally through the prism of economics, which once released from government interference, would find its own balances.[194] "The central perception of Globalization is that civilization should be seen through economics and economics alone. If you add disease prevention or urbanization or preservation of identity (the characteristic of belonging somewhere) to a commercially driven view of human existence, you merely compound the confusion about how the world works. It was [Alexis] de Tocqueville in 1835 who said, "Can it be believed that the democracy, which has overthrown the feudal system and vanquished kings will retreat before tradesmen and capitalists."[195]

Already in 1972 the *Club of Rome* released a report of its projections on the predicament of mankind, the book was published and entitled *'The Limits to Growth' by Donella & Dennis Meadows.* The basic findings were that with the growth of the world's population, the excessive over-consumption in developed countries and the growth in various sectors of societies around the globe, then the world would ultimately run out of many key resources - for instance crude oil - and these limits would become the ultimate predicament for mankind.

In this world of *Globalisation* private households have to manage their private household production and are depending more and more, for instance like in Australia, on the world market instead of having the facilities to produce some goods and services at home for their own 'protection' against an insufficient money supply to buy these goods and services in times of economic downturn. Even in times of a booming economy sometimes it would be better for private households to expand their own safety net. *Aldous Huxley* has characterized the new generation of children in a world of consumerism "In my childhood we were taught to sing nursery rhymes and, in pious households, hymns. Today the little ones warble the Singing Commercials. Which is better—"Rheingold is my beer, the dry beer," or "Hey diddle-diddle, the cat and the fiddle"? "Abide with me" or "You'll wonder where the yellow went, when you brush your teeth with Pepsodent"? Who knows?"[196]

---

[193] Saul (2005), p. 3
[194] ibid., p. 18
[195] ibid., p. 35
[196] Huxley (1958), p. 283

Chapter 3

-------ɛ๑------

Private Households and Cash Economy[197]

3.1 Cash Economy

The *Black Economy* is not easy to describe and it is hard to measure as well. In addition the Black Economy has some different components and terms, which often describe the same or similar matters.

In the term informal economy is also included the barter system. Barter means the direct exchange of goods for goods, also direct exchange of services for services. *Black Market* means an illegal trading arrangement in which buyers and sellers do business at a price higher than the legally imposed price ceiling. The underground economy is the part of the economy that is purposely hidden from the view of the government in order to avoid taxes and regulations or because the goods and services being produced is illegal. Because underground economic activity is unreported, it is omitted from GDP. It includes the production and distribution of illegal drugs, production that uses illegal labour that is paid less than the minimum wage, and jobs done for cash to avoid paying income taxes. This last category might be quite large and includes tips earned by cab drivers, hairdressers, and hotel and restaurant workers.[198]

The *cash economy* can be defined as 'income that is not recorded in the books from which the tax return is prepared'. This includes non-declared business and

---

197 This chapter is mainly based on Fischer, Wolfgang Chr. & Byron, Peter & Lehnert, Günter (1999) Federal Consumption Tax (Goods & Services Tax, GST) and Impact on Consumer Expenditure in Townsville / North Queensland, Townsville, Australia and Fischer, Wolfgang Chr. & Fleming, Ian & Lehnert, Günter (2001) Goods & Services Tax (GST), Consumers' Perceptions after Introduction in Australia in July 2000, Townsville, Australia.

198 McTaggart, Douglas & Findlay, Christopher & Parkin, Michael (1999) Economics, third edition, Melbourne, Australia, p. 21

employment income derived from legal and illegal activities and includes evasion by those who keep records and lodge tax returns and those who do not.[199]

The Cash Economy Task Force of the Australian Commissioner of Taxation has emphasised that transactions involving cash payments and receipts are not in themselves illegal. What is illegal is where cash transactions are not declared for tax, social security and other purposes (child support, superannuation). Importantly, it needs to be recognised that it is also illegal to not record cash transactions.[200]

The Task Force considers that much of the non compliance in the cash economy relates to high volume, low dollar value transactions often motivated by business or individual financial survival. However, there is also some large-scale tax evasion in the cash economy. The level of tax evasion is unequally spread throughout the population and varies with type of income, amount of income and with attitudes toward laws and government. The Task Force is concerned that personal and household services (for example, childcare, appliance repairs and installations, gardening, car repairs etc) appear to be amongst the fastest growing sectors in the economy.[201] However, it is notable to bear in mind, that overall the primary purpose of the tax system is to fund schools, roads, hospitals, welfare and other government programs and community services which are designed to build a better society's welfare.

Sometimes the underground economy is called the *Informal Economy* as opposed to the Official Economy. The informal economy has many other names, e.g. underground, hidden, parallel, irregular, black, dual, cash, moonlight, submerged, twilight economies, etc, or le travail noir or Schattenwirtschaft or Lavoro sommerso.[202] The definition used for the informal economy is "GNP that because of unreporting or underreporting is not measured by official statistics"; and this equates with the definition used by the IMF.

Schneider defines the informal economy in a broad sense: all economic activities, which normally would be accounted in the GDP but for whatever reasons are not accounted in the official GDP. Definition of informal economy in a smaller sense:

---

199 Butler, David (1998) Chair, Cash Economy Task Force, Commissioner of Taxation, Improving Tax Compliance in the Cash Economy, Canberra, Australia, p. 14

200 ibid.

201 ibid.

202 Smith, Adrian (1981), p. 5

all economic activities, which basically are taxable but not declared to the Taxation Office.[203]

There have been attempts in Australia and elsewhere to measure the size of the *cash economy* in Australia but there is currently no official or reliable estimate of its size or of the revenue foregone. In its first report the Task Force commented that academic studies estimate the cash economy to be between 3.5 percent and 13.4 percent of GDP. The above estimates suggest that the cash economy denies the Australian community billions of revenue dollars each year putting essential government services such as social security and health at risk. The cash economy also imposes significant costs to the community through welfare fraud and avoidance of superannuation, worker's compensation and child support obligations. Furthermore, the *cash economy* puts honest business at a competitive disadvantage, and in some cases out of business, that is honest business is unable to compete for work with those who operate in the cash economy because of unfair price competition.[204]

The currency demand approach is one of the most commonly used approaches. It has been applied to many OECD countries, but has nevertheless been criticised on various grounds. Objections to this method are: Not all transactions in the shadow economy are paid in cash. Most studies consider only one particular factor, the tax burden, as a cause of the shadow economy. But others (such as the impact of regulation, taxpayers' attitudes toward the state, 'tax morality' and so on) are not considered, because reliable data for most countries is not available. Another weak point of this procedure, in most studies, is the assumption of the same velocity of money in both types of economies. One can argue there is already considerable uncertainty about the velocity of money in the official economy; the velocity of money in the hidden sector is even more difficult to estimate. Without knowledge about the velocity of currency in the shadow economy, one has to accept the assumption of an 'equal' money velocity in both sectors.[205]

---

203 Schneider & Enste (2000)
204 ibid., p. 15
205 Schneider (2001), p. 22

Table : The Size of the Shadow Economy in OECD Countries					
OECD-Countries	Size of the Shadow Economy (in % of GDP) using the Currency Demand Method				
	Average 1989/90	Average 1990/93	Average 1994/95	Average 1997/98	Average 1999/2000 1)
1. Australia	10.1	13.0	13.5	14.0	14.3
2. Belgium	19.3	20.8	21.5	22.5	22.2
3. Canada	12.8	13.5	14.8	16.2	16.0
4. Denmark	10.8	15.0	17.8	18.3	18.0
5. Germany	11.8	12.5	13.5	14.9	16.0
6. Finland	13.4	16.1	18.2	18.9	18.1
7. France	9.0	13.8	14.5	14.9	15.2
8. Greece	22.6	24.9	28.6	29.0	28.7
9. Great Britain	9.6	11.2	12.5	13.0	12.7
10. Ireland	11.0	14.2	15.4	16.2	15.9
11. Italy	22.8	24.0	26.0	27.3	27.1
12. Japan	8.8	9.5	10.6	11.1	11.2
13. Netherlands	11.9	12.7	13.7	13.5	13.1
14. New Zealand 2)	9.2	9.0	11.3	11.9	12.8
15. Norway	14.8	16.7	18.2	19.6	19.1
16. Austria	6.9	7.1	8.6	9.0	9.8
17. Portugal	15.9	17.2	22.1	23.1	22.7
18. Sweden	15.8	17.0	19.5	19.9	19.2
19. Switzerland	6.7	6.9	7.8	8.1	8.6
20. Spain 3)	16.1	17.3	22.4	23.1	22.7
21. USA	6.7	8.2	8.8	8.9	8.7
Unweighted Average over 21 OECD countries	13.2	14.3	15.7	16.8	16.7

Sources: Currency demand approach, own calculations (Prof. Dr. Friedrich Schneider, University of Linz, Altenbergerstraße 69, A-4040 Linz/Auhof).

1) Preliminary values; own calculations.

2) The figures are calculated using the MIMIC-method and Currency demand approach. Source: Giles (1999b).

3) The figures have been calculated for 1989/90, 1990/93 and 1994/95 from Mauleon (1998) and for 1997/98 and 1999 own calculations.

Methods to estimate the informal economy

Direct method	• Survey • Survey of tax evasion
Indirect method Via National Account	• Discrepancy between household expenditure and income • Discrepancy between actual and official unemployment rate
Monetary method	• Hard cash circulation • Hard cash circulation of large bills • Transaction volume • Hard cash demand
Physical input method	Electricity consumption
Causal method	• Soft modelling • Linear interdependent structural relationships

Source: Schneider & Enste 2000, p.17

3.2 Goods and Services Tax (GST) and Tax Evasion and Avoidance

Obviously it is not politically popular to reveal, among other factors, issues of tax avoidance as a matter of GST and its contribution to the size of the cash economy. In Germany the estimation of the cash economy is based on the concept of measuring the hard cash circulation, i.e. there is more hard cash in circulation than is supposed to be via recorded transactions in GDP. However, the hard cash circulation in Germany has increased in particular after the iron wall to East Europe had fallen. In East European countries including Russia there is a wide circulation of DM currency, estimated 30% to 40% of the German cash economy. Furthermore it has to be taken into account that a lot of cash economy activities would have not occurred if the consumer had to pay for it with tax and receipt. For example: Half of the houses in the State of Rhineland would have not been built if the neighbour help was not available for the 'private building' of the local people.

In almost all studies it has been found that the increase of the tax and social security contribution burdens is one of the main causes for the increase of the shadow economy.[206] The effects may be enormous once a new tax, in particular the introduction of a broad based consumption tax (VAT, GST) as an indirect tax, had been imposed as a new tax burden. For Canada, *Spiro* expected similar reactions of people facing an increase in indirect taxes and after the introduction of the GST in

[206] Schneider, Friedrich (2001), p.16

1991 – in the midst of a recession – the individuals suffering economic hardship because of the recession turned to the cash economy, which led to a substantial loss in tax revenue. "Unfortunately, once this habit is developed, it is unlikely that it will be abandoned merely because economic growth resumes".[207] When the rate of taxation is relatively high, and acts itself as an incentive for evasion and if avoidance and evasion prevail to a significant degree, public revenue can fall to an extent which either cuts public expenditure or raises the public borrowing requirements so that the developments in the cash economy affects the macro-economic policies of the Government.[208]

Caragata & Giles, who analysed the cash economy and tax evasion in New Zealand, argue that the cash economy poses a serious threat to both fiscal and monetary policy, as well as to respect for the law and the associated tax evasion leads to an increasing degree of cynicism about the role and power of government. "It also reduces public support for the philosophy of 'voluntary compliance' – the basis for the stability of the tax system in many democratic societies".[209]

It is noteworthy that *Piggott & Whalley* argue that the introduction of broadly based indirect taxes (GST) could be of benefit for the poor by participation in the cash economy.[210] Traditional wisdom comes to the conclusion that the introduction of a broad based indirect tax leads to welfare worsening of low-income earners, the unemployed and poor people in a society. However *Piggott & Whalley* stressed that in a typical base broadening exercise, newly taxed commodities (services, such as haircuts, garden care, house repair) are easier to provide from within the household than is true for previously taxed commodities (manufactures).[211] Subsequently the poor may undertake such cash activities, selling their services and home made products to the rich people in tax-free informal sector markets.

However, there is much more research to be undertaken to investigate the whole informal or cash economy, in particular from a consumption perspective. There seems to be very little known about it and the sense is that it is becoming more and more important, especially for some of the economically disadvantaged. Weekend markets with people selling vast arrays of materials from car boots are huge business in the UK, and most likely in Australia and New Zealand as well. There has been some discussion about them because of the amount of bootleg

---

207 Spiro (1993), p. 255
208 Smith (1981), p. 11
209 Caragata & Giles (1998), p. 14
210 Piggott & Whalley (1998), p. 1
211 ibid., p. 2

CD's, pirate software etc. sold through those outlets but very little is known about their importance, or the types of people who choose to buy through, let alone any problems with consumer protection.[212]

It is widely recognised that one major effect of income and consumption taxation is to stimulate activities in the underground or *cash economy*. On the contrary there is little known about the factors determining the demand for goods and services produced in this sector.[213] One can expect that individuals working in the underground sector are more likely to be underground consumers than individuals who do not work in the underground sector. This would generate a positive correlation between changes in the supply and changes in the demand of goods and services in the underground sector. In this event, one expects that an increase in marginal tax rates, which encourages more people to work in the underground sector, will have a larger impact on the size of the underground sector than otherwise. Conversely, the negative effects of enforcement policies, that is more severe controls or larger penalties on tax evaders, on the importance of the underground sector will be enhanced.[214]

Fortin & Lacroix & Montmarquette show a number of reasons why individual hours of work and purchases in the underground sector are likely to be positively related. First the underground workers benefit from the information available to them. Second, preferences over goods and services in the underground sector may be non-separable from labour supply in that sector. Third, the income effect of working in the underground sector may increase the demand for some undeclared goods and services (e.g. baby-sitting services). Fourth, some people may be engaged in barter of goods and services produced informally for home consumption. Finally, unobservable individual characteristics may influence both consumption and labour supply in the underground sector in the same direction (e.g. low level of morality, dissatisfaction with government intervention, culture of tax evasion, etc.).[215] With their survey, which was conducted in 1994 in the Province of Quebec, Canada, and included over 5,000 adults 18 years and over, they provide strong evidence in support of a positive correlation between purchases of irregular commodities and hours of work in the irregular sector.

Several theories explain the relationships between paid labour in the market sector and the public sector and paid or unpaid work in the household sector.

---

[212] Lawson (2001)
[213] Fortin & Lacroix & Montmarquette (1997), p. 3
[214] ibid.
[215] ibid.

However, in pre-modern times the household sector dominated the economy. During the industrial revolution the market sector emerged and the public sector grew. In the post-industrial era the household sector is important again, because during a recession the unemployed become more active in household production, thus partly compensating for the decrease of purchasing power.

Within any tax is the creation of its evasion as far as the history of taxes leads to. GST evasion is a mutual benefit for retailers, tradespersons, servicepersons etc and the consumer as the final taxpayer of the GST. The first category of persons saves paying income tax whereas the consumer saves paying the GST. This tax evasion is much more lucrative than before the GST was introduced, because the consumer was dependent on the deduction the retailer etc calculated for him. For example, a large proportion of Australians is attracted to gambling on pokies, cards, roulette, horses, dogs etc. Avoiding the GST is an element of Australian attitudes towards gambling, a game with the Tax Office and the tax obligation. To get away with not paying GST, a widely not accepted tax, is a win of this ongoing game and not regarded as a serious criminal offence in the sense of tax fraud. GST avoidance is a different matter, that is to switch from taxed to non taxed goods and services, for example to buy basic food for home cooking or buying taxed goods but providing the necessary services by do-it-yourself. However, *Giles & Caragata* argue correctly that "tax evasion is a learned process that is shaped simultaneously by the cost savings in the opportunities to evade and the constraints and related penalties against such illegal activity".[216]

Wiegand & Rothengatter argue on the basis of anecdotal evidence "that the 'increased visibility' of the GST, as it were, may constitute an extra incentive for certain transactions, such as those which contain a high component of labour-costs (e.g. repairs/renovations by trades-people and domestic services), to be done on a 'No-Invoice-Required' basis".[217] Many of these so-called 'moonlighting' jobs are characterised by flexible schedules and appear to be those in which there is high absenteeism, where little training is provided by the firm or the private household, where self employment is prevalent, and union coverage is minimal. A reduction in the income tax rate applicable to labour earnings or the reality of the GST is not necessarily likely to enhance the supply of labour in this second-job sector.

The growth in the cash economy can be demonstrated moreover with the ratio of total amount of hard cash circulation measured as a percentage of the GDP.

[216] Giles & Caragata (1999)
[217] Wiegand & Rothengatter (2000), p. 98

Given the same velocity of hard cash and even the same mode of non-cash payments over the period January 1998 to April 2001, then the increased percentage of hard cash in circulation as a percentage of the GDP indicates the growth of the cash economy.

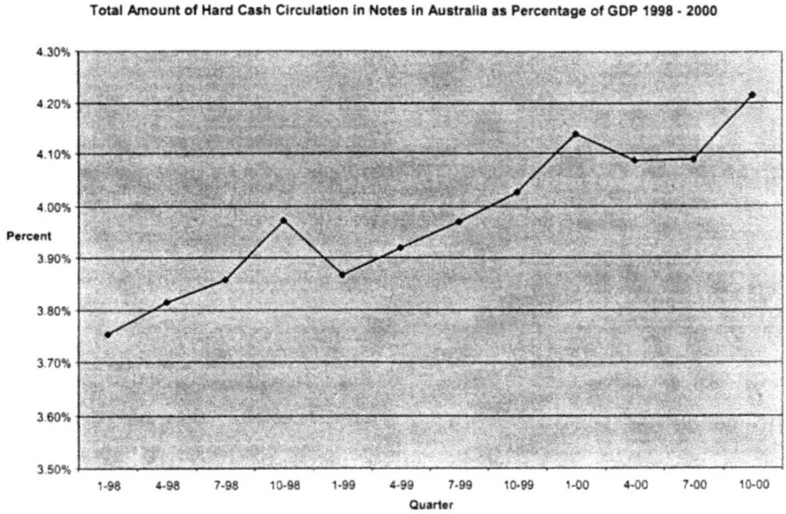

Source: RBA 2001 & ABS 2001
Note: The inflated GDP of the relevant year versus quarterly total amount of hard cash circulation in notes has been chosen as ratio.

Value Added Tax (VAT) was introduced in the *European Economic Community* in 1970 by the first and second VAT directives and was intended to replace the production and consumption taxes, which had hitherto been applied by the Member States. The cumulative effect of these cascade taxes was to create a barrier to trade, particularly imports and exports between Member States, as it was difficult to calculate the exact amount of tax incorporated in the price of goods and services. *VAT*, on the other hand, has the advantage of making the tax content of a product visible at each stage in the production or distribution chain. It was chosen as a method of indirect taxation because it avoided the cumulative effect of cascade taxes and ensured tax neutrality both nationally and in trade between Member States and with non-Community countries.[218]

VAT Rates applied in the Member States of the European Community
Situation at 1st May 1999

Member States	Standard Rate in % and dates		Reduced Rate in % 1999	VAT Rate in % Foodstuffs 1999
Belgium	18 21	1971 1999	6	6
Denmark	10 25	1967 1999	9.25	25
Germany	10 16	1968 1999	7	7
Greece	18 18	1987 1999	8	8
Spain	12 16	1986 1999	6 7	4
France	16.66 20.6	1968 1999	5.5	5.5
Ireland	16.37 21	1972 1999	12.5	0
Italy	12 20	1973 1999	10	4
Luxembourg	8 15	1970 1999	6	3
Netherlands	12 17.5	1969 1999	6	6
Austria	16 20	1973 1999	10/12	10
Portugal	16 17	1986 1999	5/12	5
Finland	22 22	1994 1999	8/17	17
Sweden	11.11 25	1969 1999	6/12	12
United Kingdom	10 17.5	1973 1999	5	0

Source: *European Commission, Directorate General XXI, Division Customs and Indirect Taxation, XXI/900/98-EN, Brussels 1999.*

VAT is a general consumption tax, which is directly proportional to the price of goods and services. It is collected fractionally, i.e. on each transaction in the economic chain, and is neutral. It is a general tax applying in principle to all

[218] European Commission (1999), p. 12

commercial activities involving the production and distribution of goods and provision of services. It is a consumption tax because it is borne ultimately by the final consumer. It is not a charge on companies. It is charged, as a percentage of price, which means the actual tax burden is visible at each stage in the production and distribution chain. It is collected fractionally, via a system of deductions whereby taxable persons (i.e. VAT-registered businesses) can deduct from their VAT liability the amount of tax they have paid to other taxable persons on purchases for their business activities. This mechanism ensures the tax is neutral regardless of how many transactions are involved.[219]

The introduction of the *VAT* standard rate in the *European Union* varies between 1967 (Denmark) and 1994 *(Finland)*. However it is obvious that in most countries of the *European Union* the *VAT* standard rate was introduced on a level around 10% and then has been increased significantly over the following years. The highest VAT standard rate applies to Denmark and Sweden with 25 percent in 1998. Apart from the VAT standard rate applying for the overwhelming majority of goods and services, the VAT reduced rate applies to foodstuff, water supplies, pharmaceutical products, medical equipment, transport of passengers, books, newspapers, periodicals, social housing, hotel accommodation, admission to sporting events, cremation services, medical and dental care, etc. The reduced rate varies between the items listed above. In most member states of the *European Union* foodstuffs are either not taxed or on a VAT reduced rate. VAT evasion also takes place in the so-called black labour market, or in other words in the demand and supply of services provided in the cash economy. Within the European Union Italy and Greece have the largest cash economies, each generating about 30 per cent of gross domestic product, according to a report by the Italian research institute *Eurispes*. The report said Italy's off-the-books economy was worth about 530 trillion lire (about A$400 million).[220] According to *Orseu*, the cash economy accounts for between 20 and 25 per cent of GDP in Italy, 4 to 6 per cent in Germany, 6 to 10 per cent in France and 8 to 12 per cent in the United Kingdom in 1994.[221] In 1996 *ISTAT* estimated a total of 10.7 million non-regular employment positions in Italy, an increase with respect to the previous survey and corresponding to 37 per cent of total employment positions in the economy.[222]

The Danish Government considered by the end of the 20th century to abolish the VAT with the standard rate of 25 percent on such services like home repair, car

---

219 European Commission (1999), p. 13
220 Papuc, Andrea (2000), p. 11
221 Orseu (1995)
222 Brunetta, Renato & Ceci, Anna (1998), pp. 257-289

repair, hairdressing, electrical appliances repair, home-building and domestic services to reduce the cash economy in these areas where cash economy activities are fairly high.[223] The consequence is that consumers will receive an incentive to order these services from business, which will implement these services in their bookkeeping for income and corporate tax purposes.

Regular and non-regular employment in Italy 1996 (thousands of positions)

Sector	Non-regular	Regular	Total
Agriculture	4,946	468	5,414
Industry excl. constr.	659	4,399	5,058
Construction	700	1,000	1,700
Market services	3,834	8,170	12,004
Non-market services	551	3,901	4,452
Total	10,690	17,938	28,628
Of which employees	3,511	13,303	16,814

Source: Brunetta & Ceci 1998, 257-289

Spiro had delivered an excellent analysis about the relation of the introduced *GST* and the cash economy for Canada. His research results indicate that there has, in all likelihood, been a substantial increase in unreported economic activity, coinciding exactly with the introduction of the *GST*.[224] Like the Australian Government argued later, the Canadian Government tried to convince the taxpayers that this value added tax might reduce the scope for tax evasion, because it applied successively at different stages of processing, and therefore to claim tax credits from the previous stage a large number of unregistered business will register for tax purposes. However, this effect might be exaggerated due to the fact that most business required tax invoices for income tax documentation. It is correct that "in practice, most businesses are not so foolhardy as to attempt to evade all taxes. They choose some fraction of their sales that they do not report. They then claim their whole input tax credit against the portion of their sales that they do report, and so they do not lose any input tax credits through GST evasion. Of course, service providers of this type have always had a large incentive to underreport their sales in order to evade income taxes".[225] Consequently, the introduction of the GST gives their customers an additional incentive to pay cash and be a party to the tax evasion.

223 Heinesen (1999), p. 235
224 Spiro, Peter S. (1993), pp. 247-258
225 ibid.

There is no doubt that if a retailer operates to an extreme, Revenue Canada will be alerted. On the contrary if a retailer underreports sales by a mere 5 to 10 percent it is unlikely to arouse suspicion in a simple computer audit.[226] Anecdotal evidence from European countries leads to the conclusion that in Canada as well "tax evasion is most prevalent in businesses that are small enough that the owner or a member of his or her family can do the bookkeeping".[227] Given that only 75,000 businesses had to be controlled for the Manufacturers Sales Tax (MST) prior to the introduction of the GST, then Revenue Canada has to monitor since 1991 roughly 1,5 million businesses under the GST regime. Obviously there is enough room for potential tax evaders to escape an audit.

In the case of Canada, *Spiro* asserts that "there was an increase in the underground economy in 1991 owing to the GST".[228] Notably there has been a remarkable increase in cash balances relative to reported expenditures, and "there does not appear to be any viable explanation of this observation other than the conclusion that the underground economy has grown".[229] *Smith* reports that Statistics Canada estimated the size of the underground economy in Canada to be probably between 1 and 5 percent of GDP,[230] whereas *Schneider* estimated the size of the Shadow Economy (in % of GDP), using the Currency Demand Method, to be 12.8% in 1989/1990 and increasing in 1999/2000 to 16.0%.[231] Obviously there are differences in using various methods to calculate the cash economy, which overall is revealed as being a difficult task by all means. However, *Spiro* had chosen the large increase in cash in circulation relative to reported incomes as evidence for the increase of the cash economy due to the GST being introduced in Canada.[232] Nevertheless, this evidence has to be taken cautiously. First of all, one can assume that the velocity of circulation and hoarding of hard cash might be higher in the underground economy due to the nature of business transactions.

Flexman, formerly with Revenue Canada as Deputy Director General for GST Policy and Legislation, had undertaken a survey of Canadian taxpayers and their attitudes towards taxation in 1994.[233] The survey was national in scope, with respondents randomly chosen from different regions to ensure representativeness of the Canadian population. Some 1,025 Canadians were contacted by telephone

---

226 Spiro, Peter S. (1993), pp. 247-258
227 ibid.
228 ibid.
229 ibid.
230 Smith, Philip (1997), p. 16
231 Schneider, Friedrich (2001), p. 112
232 Spiro, Peter S. (1997), pp. 18-27
233 Flexman, Bruce (1997), pp. 27-37

during the week January 31 to February 5, 1994.[234] Horrendous survey results were presented: "Some 86 percent of Canadians believe that governments squander a lot of the money they collect in taxes. Less than one quarter of Canadians could be categorised as 'model citizens'. Half of our respondents were categorised as 'upset and envious' or 'tax anarchists'."[235] Ultimately *Flexman* exposed that the survey "indicated a surprisingly high social acceptance of tax evasion".[236]

Relation between the Underground Economy and Taxes as a Share of GDP

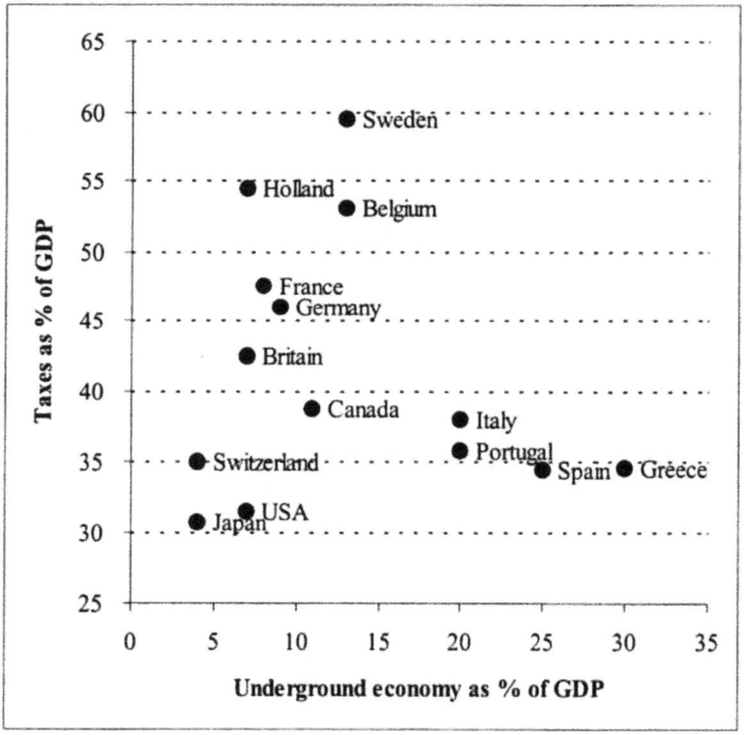

Source: Spiro, Peter S. (1997), Taxes, Deficits, and the Underground Economy

234 Flexman, Bruce (1997), pp. 27-37
235 ibid.
236 ibid.

Lehnert analysed the underground economy and the tax system for *Germany* in 2001.[237] The worldwide accepted system of national accounting is the conceptual framework for the description of economies based on the division of labour and collects in numerical values the interdependent streams of transactions undertaken in past and present. The reported figures tell us plausible stories of mankind's struggle for existence and the fight against scarcity. Are these stories true? From a non-committed perspective one might take as a starting point for the discussion:

- The official statistics neglect parts of the production and consumption of goods and services in their accounting concepts.
- The reported figures do not tell the full story on economic efforts (inputs) and their results (outputs): gross domestic income (GDI) and gross domestic product (GDP) – the largest-scale values – are higher than officially calculated.
- The underground economy is the 'visible' result of the 'invisible' hand, the (black) market outcome of demand and supply and the revealed preferences of the participants.[238]

The results of the currency demand approach in the following figure report on the underground economy in a broad and a narrow sense, both as a share of GDP. The underground economy is the fastest growing sector in Germany. Its share in GDP has nearly tripled in the last 25 years. Comparing it internationally Germany ranges in the (low) middle of OECD countries and the members of the European Union. The Mediterranean nations (Spain, Portugal, Italy, and Greece) have a longer tradition in underground activities and seem to value it less harmful.[239]

The '*Soziale Marktwirtschaft*' (social market economy) is the guideline for the economic order of the Federal Republic of Germany since the money reform in 1948 and the introduction of the Deutschmark (DM). It is a compromise of liberal and social ideas, emphasising the efficiency of the market, but respecting limits to tolerable inequality (efficiency versus equity). 'Soft' industrial relations worker's participation in the management of 'big business' was legally introduced – a successful experiment.[240] The basic lines of the concept have not changed after reunification of West- and East Germany in 1991. In the private and public mix of the national economy government's objectives are efficient resource allocation (public goods production), more equal income redistribution than 'pure' market economies and economic stability (prices and cycles). The evaluation of the objectives was liberal at the beginning, became more state-interventionist

[237] Lehnert, Günter (2001), p. 80
[238] ibid.
[239] ibid., p. 83
[240] ibid.

(socialistic) in the early 1970s and goes back to deregulation and privatisation in the 1990s. This is quantitatively reflected in public shares in GDP and GDI. Most forecasts expect diminishing shares in the near future. If it is not just marginal, it may serve as an instrument against the trend of a growing underground economy.[241]

Underground (Shadow) Economy in Germany[1]

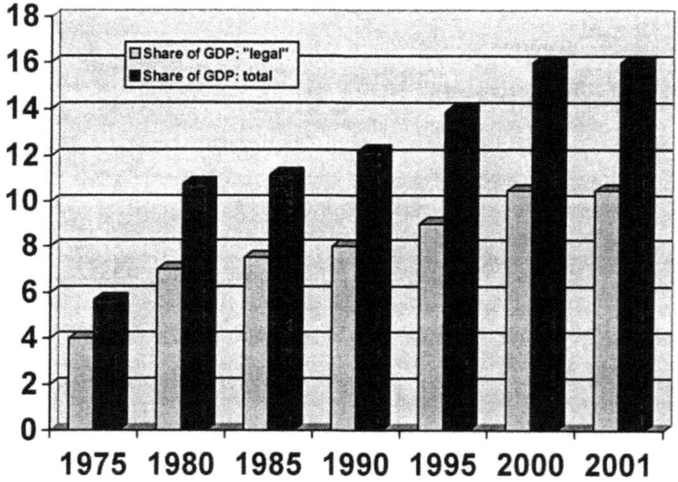

Note: The first column includes cash flows on criminal transactions (eg. drug production and distribution); the second summarises legal, but disguised business (Schattenwirtschaft versus Schwarzarbeit). The latter is about two thirds of the total share.
Source:[1] Enste, Dominik H., Schattenwirtschaft und Schwarzarbeit – Eine wirtschafts- und gesellschaftspolitische Herausforderung, in: Perspektiven der Wirtschaftspolitik, 2, 2001, p. 229-244

[241] Lehnert, Günter (2001), pp. 83-84

Government's Shares in Germany
In %

Year	Taxes	Taxes and Social Security	Expenditures (Social Security included)
1960	21,0	31,0	35,0
1970	22,9	32,9	38,1
1980	25,1	38,2	48,9
1990	22,9	36,7	50,6
2000 [1]	22,5	36,0	49,0

[1] provisional
Source: Calculations from data of the Statistiches Bundesamt, Wiesbaden, selected years

Regimentation of the labour market and the tax-included price of labour are regarded as the main causes of 'black work' *(Schwarzarbeit)* in Germany, that is working hours per week, minimum wage rates low flexibility in working time, high unemployment, and early retirement alimentation of unemployed people. If this holds true then deregulation and lower taxation on labour would be an additional instrument to push the underground economy. Or to put it in a smooth way: We shall increase the incentives to convert illegal into legal labour.[242] The underground economy reduces the input costs of labour in production and the prices of labour-intensive outputs by the amount of tax avoidance (contributions to social security included). In actual fact, unofficial estimations calculate the amount of the black market wage rate as just one third of the regular wage rate. The risk of detection and punishment for this illegal behaviour differs between direct and indirect taxation. *VAT* (GST), which has a lot of advantages, has the weakness to be easier avoidable compared to income taxation.[243]

Lehnert concludes: "From a moral point of view the world-wide observable trend towards fast growing underground economies may be valued as an increase in illegally and dishonest behaviour which cannot be tolerated and has to be persecuted tooth and nail. From an economic point of view this is rational as long as the marginal benefits of reduced tax evasion are above the marginal costs of control and punishment. In *Germany* with a share of 16% of the underground economy in GDP it seems more appropriate and valuable to convert illegal (not criminal and

---

242 Lehnert, Günter (2001), pp. 83-84
243 ibid.

organised) activities into legal ones: One should reduce incentives for dishonest behaviour of the citizen. The most effective instruments seem to be deregulation (especially in labour markets) and reduction of public duties. The shape of *VAT* with reduced or zero rates on necessities were introduced to reduce the regressive effects on consumption and low income. Reduced rates on labour-intensive production, as recommended by the *European Union* (EU) to her member states, go in the same direction and would minimise at the same time the incentives for illegal handling of legal transactions. For liberal citizens the burden of less tax income is an enforced incentive of the sovereign to his government to economise his funding and spending behaviour."[244]

[244] Lehnert, Günter (2001), p. 86

Chapter 4

-------ဢ------

Private Households and Economic Inflation[245]

4.1 History of Economic Thought about Inflation at the Turn of the 20th Century

> "The history of economic thought has a twofold function; to explain the past and to help us to understand the present. By examining the economic theories of the past we can learn to see the problems of earlier times, as it were, through the eyes of their contemporaries. By comparing them with the theories of the present we can realize better the implications and the limitations of the knowledge of our own day."[246]

Inflation has an extensive notation within the History of Economic Thought Going back even to the Medieval Ages and the *Scholasticism* some aspects of inflation were a matter of concern. *St. Thomas Aquinas*, the most important of the scholastic writers, attempted to reconcile the religious teachings of the Catholic Church with the slowly increasing economic activity of the time.

In his time the medieval Catholic Church was concerned that increasing economic activities would turn the minds and hearts of humans from religious and ethical affairs and toward materialism.[247] *St. Thomas Aquinas* and other scholastics were less interested in analysing the formation of prices in an economy including the role that prices play in the allocation of scarce resources, but more focused on the ethical aspects of prices, that is discussing issues of equity and justice. The basic question was whether religious doctrine forbade merchants to sell goods for more than they paid or for tradespeople to charge more for their services than their

---

245 This chapter is based on Chapter 5 Hyperinflation 1922/1923 in the book Fischer, Wolfgang Chr. (2010) German Hyperinflation 1922/23 – A Law and Economics Approach, Eul Verlag, Köln, Germany

246 Robbins (1937), p. xi

247 Landreth & Colander (2002), p. 37

labour costs – in other words the religious and moral area under discussion was whether taking profits and interest were sinful acts? "Thus, the scholastic concept of just price is seen alternatively as a forerunner of the *Ricardian-Marxian* labour theory of value…and the notion implicit in classical-neoclassical theory that competitive markets yield ideal just prices".[248]

St. Thomas Aquinas (1227–1274)[249]

In *Adam Smith's* famous book 'An Inquiry into the Nature and Causes of the Wealth of Nations' (1776) he affirmed that markets are the *invisible hands* to produce the best outcome from economic interactions. Smith was concerned about the new economic order, which should be replacing the state intervention within the economic order of mercantilism at his time in England. He drew his major policy conclusion from his stated facts that human beings are rational, have astute powers of judgment and are driven by *self-interest.* If they are left alone each individual will follow its self-interest, and in promoting self-interest support the interests of society. Therefore governments should not interfere by imposing regulations and can consequently follow a policy of *laissez faire.* Smith conceded that markets often fail to produce ideal social results, but current reality convinced him that the results

248 Landreth & Colander (2002), p. 38
249 http://en.wikipedia.org/wiki/St._Thomas_Aquinas

of government intervention were less acceptable than those flowing from free markets.[250] *Adam Smith* advocated *laissez faire,* but he was also aware that markets do not always produce the best outcome for the society. However, inflation in a broader sense was a matter of less concern, only price inflation could be seen as a matter of interest. However, the classical economists were very exact in defining economic terms, because they were constructing a language on which an emerging science was being built. "Among their first contributions was to make explicit the distinction between 'real' and 'nominal' prices. A good's real price, or *value,* was defined as the effort required to produce it, while its nominal, or *money,* price was said to be its cost in money alone (fixed in terms of gold or some other precious metal)".[251] Therefore the value of goods is attached by the laws of nature and the effort of labour, but their nominal price fluctuates with the availability of the precious metal, and the laws of the *Sovereign,* that define a nation's money.[252] "The real price of everything...is the toil and trouble of acquiring it. The same real price is always of the same value; but on account of the variations in the value of gold and silver, the same nominal price is sometimes of very different values".[253]

Adam Smith (1723-1790)[254]

[250] Landreth & Colander (2002), p. 38

[251] Bryan (1997), p, 1

[252] ibid.

[253] Smith, Adam (1776)

[254] http://en.wikipedia.org/wiki/Adam_Smith

Karl Marx and his collaborator *Friedrich Engels* contrary to the often expressed public opinion that both had written about how a socialist or communist economy should be built – had only a few ideas about a communist society, which were published in *The Communist Manifesto* in 1848. The Communist Manifesto (Some selected elements of a Classless Society):

- Abolition of property in land and application of all rents of land to public purposes;
- Abolition of all right of inheritance;
- Equal liability of all to labour;
- Free education for all children in public schools;
- Abolition of children's factory labour in its present form.

Das kommunistische Manifest (1848)[255]
Karl Marx & Friedrich Engels

255 (The Communist Manifesto) 'Proletarians of the World Unite!'

Karl Marx analysed in his famous book Das Kapital – Kritik der politischen Ökonomie (The Capital) 1867, a treatise against the laissez faire of *Adam Smith* and *David Ricardo,* about the underlying principles and mechanism of capitalism in detail, embedded in a precise study of the economic and social history of mankind and the antagonism of the integration of the new working class into the newly formed industrial society, but analysing the phenomenon of inflation was not a concern. On the whole *Karl Marx* was a protagonist of a communist society, which would bring an end to all the misery of the class struggle. "And just as for post-millennial Christians, man, led by God's prophets and saints, would establish a Kingdom of God on Earth (and, for pre-millennial, *Jesus* would have many human assistants in establishing such a Kingdom), so for *Marx* and other schools of communists, mankind, led by a vanguard of secular saints, would establish a secularized kingdom of heaven on earth".[256]

Karl Marx asserted that the central driving force of capitalism was in the exploitation and alienation of labour. The ultimate source of capitalist profits and surplus was the unpaid labour of wage labourers. Employers could appropriate the new output value because of their ownership of the productive capital assets, protected by the state. By producing output as capital for the employers, the workers constantly reproduced the condition of capitalism by their labour.[257] He explained the objective '*laws of motion*' of the *capitalist system* as a whole, its origins and future. His aims were to reveal the causes and dynamics of the accumulation of capital, the growth of wage labour, the transformation of the workplace, the concentration of capital (the expropriation of the expropriators), competition, the banking and credit system, the tendency of the rate of profit to decline, land-rents and in conclusion "The worker becomes all the poorer the more wealth he produces, the more his production increases in power and range. The worker becomes an ever cheaper commodity the more commodities he creates".[258] *Karl Marx* had experienced the expansion of markets; the accumulation of capital, and that in reality the cash nexus stripped away all previous religious and political illusions, but only to replace them with another kind of illusion, the 'commodity fetishism'. *Karl Marx* predicted that in capitalism, improvements in technology and rising levels of productivity increase the amount of material wealth in society while simultaneously diminishing the economic value of this wealth, thereby lowering the rate of profit. This is a tendency that leads to the paradox, characteristic of crises in capitalism, of 'poverty in the midst of plenty', or more precisely, crises of

---

[256] Rothbard (2006), p. 317
[257] Marx (1867)
[258] Marx (1867), Vol. 1

overproduction in the midst of under consumption.[259] Although *Karl Marx* and *Friedrich Engels* were not focused on the matter of 'inflation' in the broader sense, their analysis of the *Laissez faire* market concept and the 'laws' of capitalism laid the foundation of critical discussions about the economic and social order to be placed in a rapid growing industrialization with periods of mostly 'free trade'. It was left to later economists to study the phenomenon of 'inflation' once inflation had become an essential economic problem.

Karl Marx (1818-1883)[260]

The integration of the working class into the emerging industrial state was a matter of concern to the so-called *Kathedersozialisten* (mock name) (Socialists of the Chair) *Verein für Socialpolitik* (Association for Social Policy). This was a group of national economists who gathered in 1872 in *Eisenach*, Germany, to look for solutions to this essential social question. The *Verein für Socialpolitik* (Association for Social Policy) had an important influence on the social legislation of the *German Empire (1871-1918)*.

259 Marx (1867), Vol. 1

260 http://en.wikipedia.org/wiki/Karl_Marx

Gustav von Schmoller, Professor in Halle (1864-72), Strasbourg (1872-82), and Berlin (1882-1913) was the leading economist of *Imperial Germany.* He was the leader of the *Kathedersozialisten* and founder and long-time chairman of the *Verein für Socialpolitik.*

Gustav von Schmoller (1838-1917)

The idea that changes in the quantity of money affect only the money price of goods, not their value, was championed by many of the early classical economists, most notably *David Hume.* This theory was more rigorously developed in the early twentieth century by American economist *Irving Fisher,* and has come to be known as the 'quantity theory of money'.[261] "To these early economists, the word 'money' almost always referred to a metallic coin. But the first generation of economists following *Adam Smith* in the nineteenth century was very interested in paper money, since this form of payment had become popular in the burgeoning American colonies. The colonies offered a large variety of paper currencies, virtually all of which were conspicuous by their 'overproduction' and their subsequent rapid loss of purchasing power. The Continental Congress issued a paper note to help finance the American Revolution, and these 'bills of credit' became a circulating medium. In 1775, Congress issued $6 million of the new currency and urged the states to impose taxes for its ultimate redemption. The taxes were never raised, however, and larger continental issues were authorized. By the end of 1779, Congress had expanded the number of continental bills of credit more than 40-fold, and, to make matters worse,

[261] Bryan (1997)

the states had issued their own paper monies in a similar magnitude. In 1781, a dollar in paper was worth less than two cents in gold coin".[262]

"Inflation is the process of making addition to currencies not based on a commensurate increase in the production of goods" - Federal Reserve Bulletin 1919.[263] During the first several decades of the twentieth century the effects on the increase of the price level became more obvious for economists, because they could be certain of the 'excessiveness' of the circulating medium only by its effect on the price level, the notions of an inflated currency and prices became inextricably linked.[264] "Linking *inflation* to the price level proved to be another important turning point for the world. With the publication of *John Maynard Keynes'* General Theory in 1936, an assault on the quantity theory of money commenced, and it dominated macroeconomic thought for the next forty years. "By appealing to the belief that resources could be regularly and persistently under employed, an idea given support by the worldwide depression of the time, *Keynesian* theory challenged the necessary connection between the quantity of money and the general price level. Moreover, it suggested that aggregate price increases could originate from factors other than money. In addition to separating the price level from the money stock, the Keynesian revolution in economics appears to have separated the word *inflation* from a condition of money and redefined it as a description of prices. In this way, inflation became synonymous with any price increase. Indeed, Keynes spoke about different 'types' of inflation, including income, profit, commodity, and capital inflation".[265]

Keynes takes a tough attitude in his *Economic Consequences of the Peace (1919*, condemning inflation in the harshest possible way.[266] *Keynes* came to the conclusion: "*Lenin* is said to have declared that the best way to destroy the capitalist system was to debauch the currency. By a continuing process of inflation, governments can confiscate, secretly and unobserved, an important part of the wealth of their citizens. By this method they not only confiscate, but they confiscate arbitrarily; and, while the process impoverishes many, it actually enriches some. He agrees with *Lenin* that inflation has the potentiality of destroying the basis of capitalist society. *Lenin* was certainly right. There is no subtler, no surer means of overturning the existing basis of society than to debauch the currency".[267] *Keynes*' concern with the

262 Bryan (1997)
263 ibid.
264 ibid.
265 ibid.
266 Humphrey (1981), p. 4
267 ibid.

dangers of inflation influenced his policy advice in the post-war boom of 1920 when an outburst of inflation threatened the British economy. "Keynes' advocacy of tight money in this episode clearly rested on his fear of the damage that continuing rapid inflation could inflict on society and the capitalist system. He stated as much in a memorandum written shortly after his meeting with the Chancellor of the Exchequer. He feared that persistent inflation would generate social unrest and strike at the whole basis of contract, of security, and of the capitalist system generally, eventually leading to socialistic control over industry."[268]

John Maynard Keynes (1883-1946)[269]

At the turn of the 20th century the *American Institutionalist School,* commonly associated with *Thorstein Bunde Veblen* (1857-1929) and *Wesley Clair Mitchell* (1874-1948), was for a short period dominant in the *United States.* The *American Institutionalist School* was developed in the late 1880s in the United States and was heavily influenced by the *German Historical School* and the *English Historicists.* They asserted that much in the economic world was not immutable but rather conditioned by the influence of an always changing history - whether acting on the individual directly, or indirectly through the institutions and society which surround him.[270] It was then *John Kenneth Galbraith,* who presented in his famous book *The Affluent Society* (1958) a harsh critic of the American's private wealth and materialism in the sense of 'private wealth versus public poverty'.

---

268 Humphrey (1981), p. 5
269 http://en.wikipedia.org/wiki/John_Maynard_Keynes
270 Stavro (2006), p. 26

Galbraith argued that the free market economy was a myth and that the 1000 largest American corporations dominated both the nation's economy and social life. Giant corporations essentially operated free of competition, often turning out frivolous goods for an ever increasingly consumer-minded society, while the capitalistic economy ignored more pressing social needs.[271] He tried to advocate for a substantial support of the poor and he favoured intervention by the government to rein in corporate power, while using more tax money to better social needs, such as improving education and protecting the environment.[272]

John Kenneth Galbraith (1908-2006)[273]

It is worth mentioning that in the current world-wide financial crisis, which is connected with the gigantic granting of credit, the money creation by banks and the acceptance of *fiat money,* that is notes which are not worth as much as paper or metal, but are said by the government to have a value, *Karl Marx's* observations on the financial crisis of 1857, on the 'Roving Cavaliers of Credit' was recently quoted by *Steve Keen:* "Talk about centralisation! The credit system, which has its focus in the so-called national banks and the big money-lenders and usurers surrounding them, constitutes enormous centralisation, and gives this class of parasites the

[271] Stavro (2006), p. 26
[272] ibid.
[273] http://en.wikipedia.org/wiki/John_Kenneth_Galbraith

fabulous power, not only to periodically despoil industrial capitalists, but also to interfere in actual production in a most dangerous manner - and this gang knows nothing about production and has nothing to do with it".[274] *Steve Keen* comes to the reasoning "that we should never have fallen for the insane notion that the financial system should be self-regulating. All that did was give the Cavaliers a licence to run amok, with the consequences we are now experiencing yet again - 150 years after *Marx* described the crisis that led him to write *Das Kapital*".[275]

4.2 Inflationary Process

> "Cheap money is a stimulant, also an intoxicant. If the dose is large enough, a substantial temporary effect can be brought about, but headaches follow. If the matter really were that simple, everybody could be an economist, and only the perversity of central banks would keep us from endless prosperity. Merchants and manufacturers will not be induced to increase borrowings, since interest on money borrowed is only one small factor in total costs. But if merchants and manufacturers will not use cheap money, speculators will".[276]

Private households would have the opportunity to partially beat the inflation within the 'free market', if they had most of the facilities to follow an intensive private household production within the relevant sections of private household production:[277] Planning of the sections of private household production involves the nutrition, internal transport, storage, shopping, household cleaning, clothing, gardening and domestic animal care, personal care of household members.

This prospect of private household production could lead to a competition for producers and service providers in the free market because the demand of private households could substantially diminish. However the current economic situation is quite different due to the majority of private households having lost the ability to countervail the inflation in the free market and public service. In particular this matter can be detrimental once a high inflation or even a hyperinflation has taken place.

---

[274] Keen (2009)
[275] ibid.
[276] Anderson, Benjamin (1930) Chief Economist of Chase National Bank, New York Times, April
[277] Fischer (1982), pp. 42-43

An explanation for the increasing price level is generally offered by the 'quantity equation' of *Irving Fisher*. This formula can be transformed to:

$$\Pr iceLevel = \frac{MoneySuppl\,y \bullet CurrencyCi\,rculationV\,elocity}{Transactio\,nNumber}$$

- The price level rises, therefore, among other things if the money supply rises (if the central bank puts in circulation, e.g., more money), currency circulation velocity and transaction number, however, unchanged remain.
- The currency circulation velocity rises; however, money supply and transaction number remain unchanged. ·
- The transaction number decreases (e.g., by disturbance of the economic cycle by disasters if suddenly the ability of delivery of goods and services diminished, but the demand remains), however, money supply and currency circulation velocity remain unchanged.[278]

Thomas Sargent breaking new ground on the subject of rational expectation argued "it is not the base supply of money that determines inflation but the velocity of its circulation, which in turn is a function of expectations".[279]

According to the *RBA Inflation Calculator*[280] the inflation in Australia is high: This tool calculates the change in cost of purchasing a representative 'basket of goods and services' over a period of time.

Inflation in Australia 1980 – 2009[281]

Year	'Basket' in $	Total Change in Cost in per cent	Average Annual Rate of Inflation in per cent
1980	1000.00	n.a.	n.a.
1985	1488.64	48.9	8.3
1990	2180.14	118.0	8.1
1995	2466.98	146.7	6.2
2000	2713.15	171.3	5.1
2005	3150.03	215.0	4.7
2009	3546.22	254.6	4.5

278 Hyperinflation; http://de.wikipedia.org/wiki/Hyperinflation

279 Ferguson (2010), p. 11

280 The results produced by the *Inflation Calculator* are intended as guides only and should not be regarded as 'official' Reserve Bank calculations. See www.rba.gov.au/calculator/

281 Reserve Bank of Australia, www.rba.gov.au/calculator/ November 2010

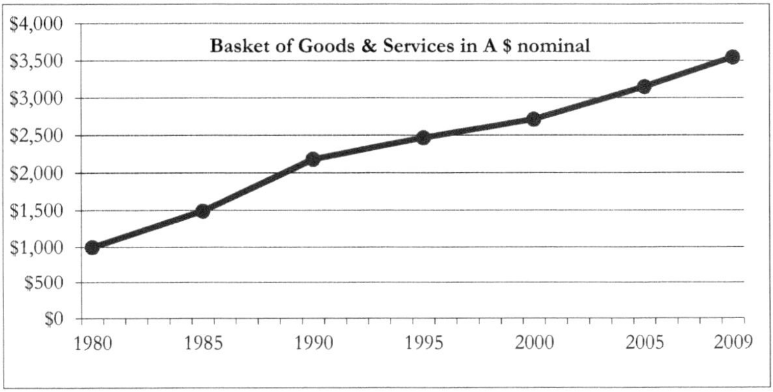

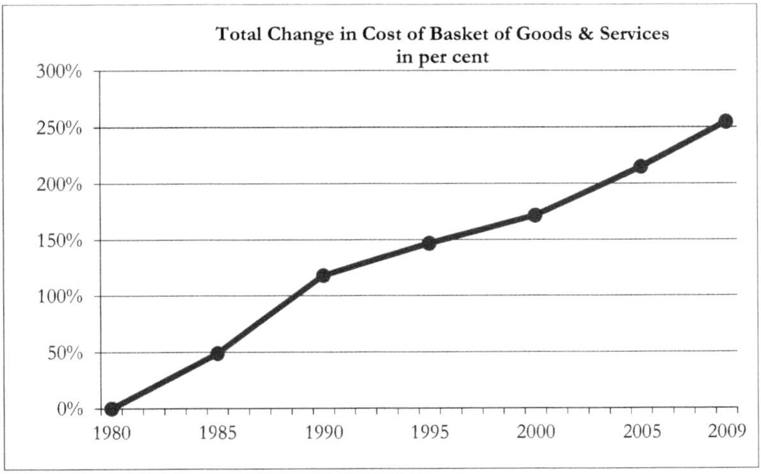

In both countries, Australia and Germany, the inflation is a permanent concern of the Governments and directly affects the private households by reducing their purchasing power.

Australian Consumer Price Index 1970 – 2009[282]

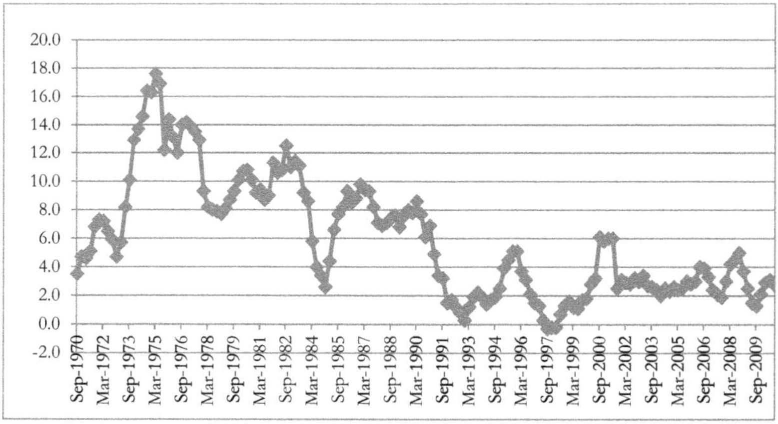

Inflation Rate in Germany 1992 - 2011[283]

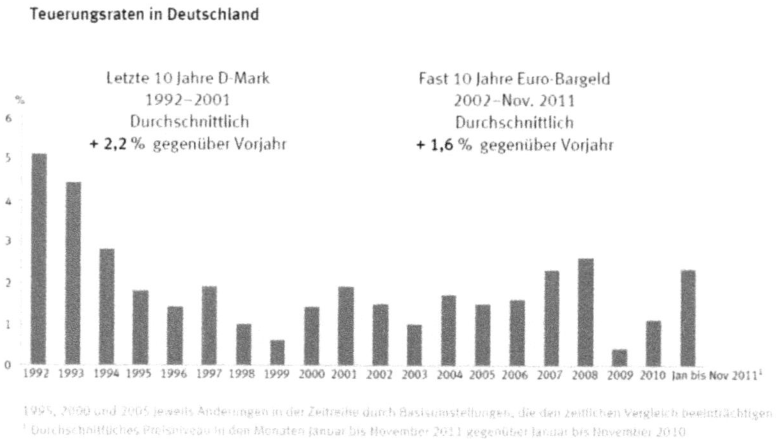

---

282 Consumer Price Index, All Groups, Year-ended percentage Change. Source: ABS, Reserve Bank of Australia, Statistical Tables, http://www.rba.gov.au/statistics/tables/index.html#prices_inflation

283 Statistisches Bundesamt (2011) Preise, Fast zehn Jahre Euro – Preisentwicklung vor und nach der Bargeldumstellung, Wiesbaden, Germany, p. 4. Note: 1992 to 2001 in DM and from 2002 to 2011 in Euro.

However, there might be a possibility that inflation with moderate to high inflation rates could glide into *Hyperinflation* and this mostly turns out to be the worst scenario for private households which have a minimum on private household production or are depleted of means to support the day to day life.

Hyperinflation is very high inflation that features a sustained increase in the aggregate price level. Although the threshold is arbitrary, economists generally reserve the term *hyperinflation* to describe episodes where the monthly inflation rate is greater than 50 percent. At a monthly rate of 50 percent, it corresponds to an annual rate of approximately 13,000 percent. Put simply, a hyperinflation is an uncontrollable inflation with extremely high monthly rates. Additionally, hyperinflation is a very *complex phenomenon*, which has its roots in not merely macroeconomic factors but also in behavioural factors of human beings. Unfortunately the arrow of time is irreversible for the period of the *German Hyperinflation* 1922/1923, or in other words, one cannot revisit the past, that is one cannot observe the actual *German Hyperinflation 1922/1923* as a complicated system at its time. Furthermore, for example when the highly complex process of hyperinflation is in the initial state of the process with a substantial variety of factors influencing each other, it cannot be regarded as mono-causal and simply deterministic. *Paul Davies* had described the basic problem involved in his work 'The Cosmic Blueprint', London 1987*,* from the viewpoint of a theoretical physicist:

> "The traditional approach to complicated, irregular systems is to model them by approximation to regular systems. The more irregular the real system is, the less satisfactory this modelling becomes...When it comes to very highly organized systems, such as a living cell, the task of modelling by approximation to simple, continuous and smoothly varying quantities is hopeless. It is for this reason that attempts by sociologists and economists to imitate physicists and describe their subject matter by simple mathematical equations is rarely convincing."[284]

In addition Davies criticised the traditional modelling in four major central themes:

> "Generally speaking, complex systems fail to meet the requirements of traditional modelling in four ways. The first concerns their formation. Complexity often appears abruptly rather than by slow and continuous evolution. Secondly, complex systems often (though not always) have a very large

---

[284] Davies (1987), p. 22

number of components (degrees of freedom). Thirdly, they are rarely closed systems; indeed, it is usually their very openness to a complex environment that drives them. Finally, such systems are predominantly 'non-linear'.[285]

Michel Baranger analysed *chaos* and *complexity* in the following way: "Lacking a precise definition, we can try to convey the meaning of complexity by enumerating what seem to be the most typical properties: Some of these properties are shared by many non-biological systems as well:

- Complex systems contain many constituents interacting nonlinearly.
- The constituents of a complex system are interdependent.
- A complex system possesses a structure spanning several scales.
- A complex system is capable of emerging behaviour.
- Complexity involves interplay between chaos and non-chaos.
- Complexity involves interplay between cooperation and competition. Once again this is interplay between scales."[286]

The American *artificial intelligence* researcher *Marvin Minsky* argued rightly:

"Many scientists look on chemistry and physics as ideal models of what psychology should be like. After all, the atoms in the brain are subject to the same all-inclusive laws that govern every other form of matter. Then can we also explain what our brains actually do entirely in terms of those same basic principles? The answer is no, simply because even if we understand how each of our billions of brain cells work separately, this would not tell us how the brain works as an agency. The 'laws of thought' depend not only upon the properties of those brain cells, but also on how they are connected. And these connections are established not by the basic, 'general' laws of physics, but by the particular arrangements of the millions of bits of information in our inherited genes. To be sure, 'general' laws apply to everything. But, for that very reason, they can rarely explain anything in particular."[287]

---

285 Davies (1987), p. 22

286 Baranger (2008), p. 11

287 Minsky, Marvin (1987) The Society of Mind, New York, p. 26, quoted by Paul Davies (1987) p. 193

In a *hyperinflation* there are many agents, for example public authorities, business, consumers, which contribute in an unpredictable way – in a *complex system* – to establish the full momentum of an inflation, and like the consumers as part of the group of agents, the 'rational' behaviour will be replaced by actions of non-consistency.

For example, consumer behaviour has been investigated in many aspects in modern times, in particular through market research and marketing analyses. However, how consumers react if an economic situation occurs with high inflation, even in a hyperinflation, this is an almost unoccupied scientific area in economics and law. Most likely consumers do not react in a reasonable rational way, more likely the majority of consumers will follow the old motto 'Save our Souls'.

Michel Baranger described in his contribution to Chaos and Complexity "There are many possible definitions of the word fractal. A very loose and general definition is this: a fractal is a geometric figure that does not become simpler when you analyse it into smaller and smaller parts. The famous *Mandelbrot set,* which is highly popular in the picture books and in the museums, is a less trivial fractal, but its definition is still amazingly simple, given the resulting complexity".[288] The 'Mandelbrot Set' of *Benoît Mandelbrot* follows the simple formula $y=x^2+c$ and has to be repeated according to a certain rule. The Mandelbrot set is a famous example of a *fractal,* which is generally "a rough or fragmented geometric shape that can be split into parts, each of which is (at least approximately) a reduced-size copy of the whole," a property called self-similarity.[289]

Because they appear similar at all levels of magnification, fractals are often considered to be *infinitely complex* (in informal terms). Natural objects that approximate fractals to a degree include clouds, mountain ranges, lightning bolts, coastlines, snowflakes, even various vegetables (cauliflower and broccoli). However, not all self-similar objects are fractals – for example, the real line (a straight Euclidean line) is formally self-similar but fails to have other fractal characteristics; for instance, it is regular enough to be described in Euclidean terms.[290] "More than 40 years ago *Benoit Mandelbrot* described the fractal structure of cotton prices and the emanating properties of fat tails and volatility clustering and *Hyman Minsky* proposed a theory for endogenous speculative bubble formation. More recently *Robert Shiller* and *Alan Greenspan* made the irrational exuberance paradigm

[288] Baranger (2008), p. 5
[289] Fractal, Wikipedia (2009)
[290] ibid.

fashionable. These all fit in the framework of *Complexity Economics*, which describes the properties that emerge from interacting agents".[291]

The fairly new thought of *Complexity Economics*[292] is in general the application of the complexity science to the dilemmas of Economics. [293] *Complexity,* chaos, catastrophe and cybernetics are embedded in this new mode of economic thought, which "rejects traditional assumptions that imply that the economy is a closed system that eventually reaches equilibrium. Instead, it views economies as open complex adaptive systems with endogenous evolution. Complex systems do not necessarily settle to equilibrium – even ideal deterministic models may exhibit chaos, which is distinct from both random (nondeterministic) and analytic behaviour".[294] "In the light of the new concepts introduced, economic systems shall no more be considered as 'naturally' inclined to achieve equilibrium states. On the contrary, economic systems - like most complex and self-organized systems - are intrinsically evolutionary systems, which tend to develop, prevailingly toward levels of higher internal organization; though the possibility of involution processes - or even of catastrophic events - remains immanent".[295] The hyperinflation may well be seen as one of these catastrophic events. Furthermore the episode of the tremendous acceleration of the inflation in Germany in 1923 could be classified as a sensitive dependence on initial conditions, which had changed substantially at that time.

It would be worthwhile to implement the inflationary process of a hyperinflation into the *Chaos Theory.* Chaos Theory studies the behaviour of those systems which appear random to the naked eye, but are in fact deterministic from a mathematical perspective in that the current state of the system fixes the system at later intervals. The inherent randomness is attributable to a concept called sensitive dependence on initial conditions whereby relatively minor variations in the initial variables can have a significant impact on future behaviour. The signature of time-chaos is something called sensitivity to initial conditions. "It says that, if you have

---

[291] Sornette (2009)

[292] See Appendix 6, Comparison with Traditional Economics, http://en.wikipedia.org/wiki/Complexity_economics.

[293] See further details of Complexity Economics:
The Santa Fe Institute (SFI) is a non-profit research institute located in Santa Fe (New Mexico, United States) and dedicated to the study of complex systems. The Santa Fe Institute was founded in 1984 by George Cowan, David Pines, Sterling Colgate, Murray Gell-Mann (American physicist who received the 1969 Nobel Prize in physics for his work on the theory of elementary particles), Nick Metropolis, Herb Anderson, Peter A. Carruthers, and Richard Slansky
Beinhocker, Eric D. (2006) The Origin of Wealth: Evolution, Complexity, and the Radical Remaking of Economics, Boston, Massachusetts: Harvard Business School Press

[294] Complexity Economics (2010)

[295] ibid.

two sets of initial conditions or two points in phase space, extremely close to each other, the two ensuing trajectories, though close to each other at the beginning, will eventually diverge exponentially away from each other. *Edward Lorenz*, the discoverer of sensitivity to initial conditions, also called it 'the butterfly effect' because, thanks to sensitivity to initial conditions, it is possible for a butterfly, by flapping its wings on some Caribbean island today, to change completely the weather pattern in Europe a month from now."[296]This interpretation underscores the difficulty associated with forecasting of chaotic systems. This difficulty has been seized upon by a number of scientists who have argued that chaos is detrimental to determinism, and the hyperinflation in Economics, in particular its accelerated process of the price level and the decay of the value of money relative to the previous purchasing power, certainly fulfil some criteria of the Chaos & Complexity Theory.

In a *hyperinflation* the interacting agents are continuously influencing each other. "In scientific literature it is said that such a system is subject to non-linear dynamics. Modelling such a system in full detail is practically impossible to do".[297] "Recent research, however, has provided new tools to analyse complex non-linear systems without having to go through the simulation of all underlying interactions. When interacting agents are playing in a hierarchical network structure very specific emerging patterns arise. Let us clarify this with an example. After a concert the audience expresses its appreciation with applause. In the beginning, everybody is handclapping according to their own rhythm. The sound is like random noise. There is no imminence of collective behaviour. This can be compared to financial markets operating in a steady-state where prices follow a random walk. All of a sudden something curious happens. All randomness disappears; the audience organizes itself in a synchronized regular beat, each pair of hands is clapping in unison. There is no master of ceremony at play. This collective behaviour emanates endogenously. It is a pattern arising from the underlying interactions. This can be compared to a crash. There is a steady build-up of tension in the system (like with an earthquake or a sand pile) and without any exogenous trigger a massive failure of the system occurs".[298] Similar argues the historian *Ferguson* "Such systems can appear to operate quite stably for some time; they seem to be in equilibrium but are, in fact, constantly adapting. But there comes a moment when complex systems 'go critical.' A very small trigger can set off a 'phase transition' from a benign equilibrium to a crisis".[299]

---

[296] Baranger (2008), p. 6
[297] Sornette (2009), pp. 1-2
[298] ibid.
[299] Ferguson (2010), p. 2.

Why was there a tremendous acceleration of the inflation in a very short time in Germany? Generally, the traditional explanation reduces the causes of *hyperinflation* completely to the financing of WW1 by means of war bonds, and the reparation payments, as well as on financing of national debts and public expenditures of the German Government after WW1.[300] "In 1922-23 Germany suffered the most famous hyperinflation of all time, and the only one to have afflicted a major industrial power this century. Both during and after the First World War the inflation was an instrument of government policy. Inflation, Keynes observes, is a form of 'taxation by currency depreciation'.[301] The rise in prices puts real commodities at the disposal of the note-issuer, who offers paper money in exchange. The inflation resulted from excessive monetary expansion via budget deficits."[302]

John Maynard Keynes intervention at the *Peace Conference in Paris* where his main interest had been in "trying to prevent Germany's compensation payments being set so high it would traumatize innocent German people, damage the nation's ability to pay and sharply limit her ability to buy exports from other countries - thus hurting not just Germany's own economy but that of the wider world". Keynes himself and the Treasury were largely excluded from formal high-level talks concerning reparations. Their place was taken by the Heavenly Twins - the Judge *Lord Sumner* and the Banker *Lord Cunliffe* whose nickname derived from the 'astronomically' high war compensation they wanted to demand from Germany. *Keynes* was forced to try to exert influence mostly from behind the scenes, but was unfortunately not successful.[303] However there is no generally accepted hypothesis why this acceleration of the *inflation* into a *hyperinflation*, particularly since August 1923, took place.[304]

The following diagram represents the decay of the value of the German currency: One can clearly observe a "strong upward curvature characterising a 'super-exponential' behaviour or a faster than exponential growth".[305] The collapse of the German currency *Mark* seemed to be inevitable and a new behaviour would

[300] Carl-Ludwig Holtfrerich, Deutsche Inflation 1914-1923, http://de.wikipedia.org/wiki/Deutsche_Inflation_1914_bis_1923

[301] Keynes, J.M (1924) A Tract on Monetary Reform, London, p. 9, p. 41

[302] Southern (1979), p. D1030

[303] Keynes-Wikipedia

[304] Davies (1987), p.203 "...I intended that the gaps left by the inadequacies of reductionist thinking should be filled by additional scientific theories that concern the collective and organizational properties of complex systems, and not by appeal to mystical or transcendent principles...."

[305] Johansen & Sornette (2001)

be on the agenda that is the introduction of a new currency the *Rentenmark* by the end of 1923 and in August 1924 the *Reichsmark*.

Until the outbreak of WW1 the *Mark* was convertible into gold, but then the convertibility was suspended to allow unrestricted expansion of the note issue. "Inconvertible paper currency (paper marks) was made legal tender by legislative fiat. The legal tender legislation established the rule that paper marks were compulsorily acceptable at their face value. The rule that payment in paper marks at their nominal value was a good legal discharge of debts was enshrined in the rule 'A mark is worth a Mark' (*Mark gleich Mark*)."[306]

This principle embodied the *nominalist view* that money has no intrinsic worth but is simply that which the state declares from time to time to be a good legal discharge of money contracts. The traditional explanation has been given by *Southern* in a shortened version and containing only the main points of the inflationary process leading to hyperinflation. "After the war a number of factors pre-disposed Germany to hyperinflation. The government had to pay both the huge internal debt contracted to pay for the war and massive reparations imposed by the Allies on Germany. These outgoings were too great to meet from taxation. The economy was weakened by the havoc of war and the loss of territories containing many of its most valuable resources and industries. This reduced the economy's taxable basis. The government lacked legitimacy in the eyes of wide sections of the population. The system therefore appeared weak and unstable, which reduced confidence in the currency. Experience of rising prices convinced people of the folly of saving and prudence of debts. They therefore spent money more rapidly thus increasing the velocity of circulation. The *Reichsbank*, convinced that inflation was the result – not the cause – of a credit-shortage, lent money to industry at rates which lagged far behind inflation".[307]

---

306 Southern (1979), p. D1030
The compulsory value of the paper mark was based on the following laws:
Bank Law of 1909 which made Reichsbank notes legal means of payment: 1 June 1909, Reichsgesetzblatt (=RGB1) 515;
Coin Law of 1914, which made coins exchangeable only for bank notes and Treasury certificates: 4 August 1914, RGB1 326;
Banknotes Law of 1914, which suspended the Reichsbank's obligation to redeem its notes in gold and obliged the Reichsbank to redeem Treasury certificates in banknotes to an unlimited extent: 4 August 1914, RGB1 347;
Bundesrat Decree of 1914, which suspended all gold-payment clauses in contracts: September 23, 1914, RGB1 417

307 ibid.

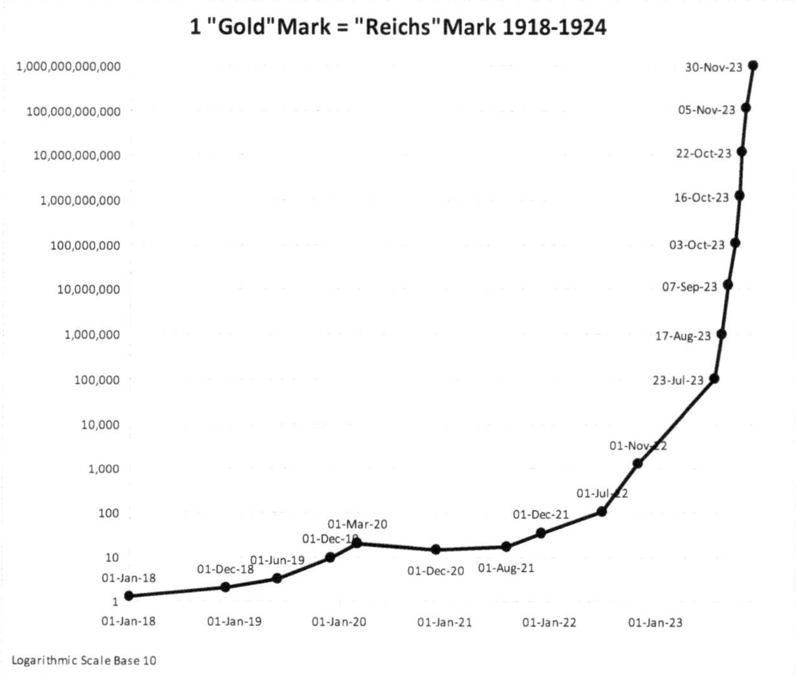

Note: 1 "Gold"Mark value in grams of fine gold (1913) = 0.35842g;
"Reichs"Mark = Currency not tied to the gold standard in 1918 to 1924.[308]

[308] Law about the Revaluation of Mortgages and other Claims (Revaluation Act 1925), issued the 16th of July, 1925, Aufwertungsgesetz, Reichsgesetzblatt, Teil I, 1925, p.133-135, and Author's calculations

Chapter 5

-------ℰ------

Self-sufficient Private Household Production Versus Money Dependency

5.1 Principles of Self-sufficient Private Household Production

The main issue of this chapter will be how private households and their private household production are embedded in a well-rounded society. The starting point could be a preference and outline of the *social market concept* which may be regarded as one of the best orders of a society in modern ages.

In all sections of *private household production*[309] there should be facilities to produce the relevant goods and services by the members of the private household simply by themselves.

- Planning of the sections of private household production
- Nutrition
- Internal transport
- Storage
- Shopping
- Household cleaning
- Clothing
- Gardening and domestic animal care
- Personal care of household members

The various sections could be illustrated with examples, for instance the questioning of *nursing homes* (Altenheim) versus taking care of elderly people at home with some outside help. Or as an example for healthy food there could be the back yard garden with some fruit trees, vegetables, berries etc. instead of having just lawn. Today, instead of food production, large TV dishes are placed in the back yard. Finally for the section of cooking there could be a more well rounded education of

---

[309] Fischer (1982), pp. 42-43

each generation in how to prepare fresh food in their 'whole form' like for instance a chicken, a whole fish, and a bunch of vegetables from the garden.

Today's 'garden'[310]

This enhanced *private household production* would lead to a reduction of market activities and obviously to a reduction in the dependence on money and income as well. All three basic categories of the integration of the private household production into the development of an economy

- *Industrialisation of private household production,*
- *Mechanisation of private household production,*
- and *Centralisation of private household production*

are affected more or less in their structure. Furthermore it would lead to a more well-rounded meaningful life and not only working under the threat of so called performance as 'human resources' in a specific area on the 'dictatorship' of companies with their essentially capitalistic behaviour and even within the institutions of the public service. The market should not be the *ultima ratio* in a well-rounded society in the sense of a *laissez-faire concept* and the only goal for private

[310] This photo had been made by the author on Magnetic Island, Australia, South Pacific

households, businesses, and governments. Furthermore there should be considered the long standing principle that the market is not suitable for all areas of maintaining and developing a society and to a certain degree public services are needed to avoid private market power, for instance in the categories of education, health, traffic, defence, police and courts. There has always been an ongoing debate within the history of economic thought about the size and structure of the *public service*. In particular in the 19th century free market advocates and their idea of a small public service were criticized by *Ferdinand Lassalle*, and he coined their nation as the 'night watchman state'. On the other hand the extension of public services to a planned economy was always the final aim of extreme orientated socialists like *Lenin*. However, during the period of the 19th and 20th century there were many economists who were advocates for a mixed economy with public service and so called free market activities which were regarded as non-antagonistic.[311] Among those many economists was *John Kenneth Galbraith,* whose main ideas focused around the influence of the market power of large corporations. He believed that this market power weakened the widely accepted principle of consumer sovereignty, allowing corporations to be price makers, rather than price takers, allowing corporations with the strongest market power to increase the production of their goods beyond an efficient amount. He further believed that market power played a major role in inflation and argued that corporations and trade unions could only increase prices to the extent that their market power allowed them to.[312] Galbraith also critiqued the assumption that continually increasing material production is a sign of economic and societal health.[313]

The basic issue of reducing poverty through the establishment of a *welfare state* within an industrialized country was raised after WWI, after the world-wide depression of the late 1920s and 1930s and finally after WWII. Then again the idea of the *welfare state* means different things in different countries.

- *Welfare state* usually refers to an ideal model of provision, where the state accepts responsibility for the provision of comprehensive and universal welfare for its citizens.
- *State welfare.* Some analysts use it to mean 'welfare provided by the state'. This is the main use in the USA.

---

311 It is not the subject of this research monograph to illustrate the various concepts within the History of Economic Thought. For a detailed History of Economic Thought see Gerhard Kolb (1997) Geschichte der Volkswirtschaftslehre, München

312 http://en.wikipedia.org/wiki/John_Kenneth_Galbraith#Economics_books

313 ibid.

- *Social protection.* In many 'welfare states', social protection is not delivered by the state at all, but by a combination of independent, voluntary and government services. These countries are still usually thought of as '*welfare states*'.

The post-war German settlement was based on the idea of a *social state*, sometimes rendered as a *social market economy*.[314] The concept of the *Social Market Economy* received fundamental impulses from reflection and critique of historical economic and social orders, namely *Smithian laissez-faire* liberalism on the one hand and *Marxian socialism* on the other. Already in the late nineteenth century, the *Kathedersozialisten* (Catheter Socialists), engaged in social reforms in the *Verein für Socialpolitik*, turned away from pure liberalism to demand a purposive state policy designed to regulate economic life and advocated a middle course between anarchic individualism, traditionalistic corporatism and bureaucratism.[315] The *Social Market Economy*[316] (*Soziale Marktwirtschaft*) is a form of market capitalism combined with a social policy favoring union bargaining and social insurance, and is sometimes classified as a coordinated market economy. Important advocates in the development of the concept include among others *Walter Eucken, Franz Böhm, Oswald von Nell-Breuning* and *Alfred Müller-Armack,* who originally coined the term *Soziale Marktwirtschaft.* They share an involvement in the Anti-National Socialist German Workers Party (NSDAP) Opposition, whose search for a post-war order for Germany is an important background for the development of this concept.[317]

Walter Eucken (1891-1950)[318]

Oswald von Nell-Breuning SJ (1890-1991)[319]

---

314 Kolb (1997), p.155
315 http://en.wikipedia.org/wiki/Social_market_economy
316 ibid.
317 ibid.
318 http://en.wikipedia.org/wiki/Walter_Eucken
319 http://de.wikipedia.org/wiki/Oswald_von_Nell-Breuning

The first, central principle was that economic development was the best way to achieve social welfare. The structure of social services had to reflect this priority. The principle is represented most clearly in the close relationship of services to people's position in the labour market. Subsequently the institution of *workers participation* (council of employees, employees on the board of directors in capital companies, employees on councils of the public services)[320] in the social and economic affairs of private companies and in the public services was introduced in the new *German Constitution*[321] of the 23rd of May 1949. The *workers participation* was established in the tradition of the *Weimar Constitution*[322] of the 14th of August 1919. The *German Constitution* of 1949 also implemented the spirit of the *Weimar Constitution* of 1919 by limiting the rights of property owners. Within the unchangeable articles of the *German Constitution* there is stated in Article 14, Section 2: "Property has responsibility. Its utilizing has to serve the common good". Furthermore in Article 20, Section 1 is codified: "The Federal Republic of Germany is a democratic and social Federal State". A *social state* can be defined as a state which aims at social security and at social justice in its action to guarantee the participation of all people in the social and political developments.

Social benefits are earnings-related, and those without work records may find they are not covered for important contingencies. But probably even more important, is the general concern to ensure that public expenditure on welfare is directly compatible with the need for economic development and growth.

Second, the German economy, and the welfare system, developed through a corporatist structure. This principle was developed by *Bismarck* on the basis of existing mutual aid associations, and remained the basis for social protection subsequently. *Social insurance*, which covers the costs of health, some social care and much of the income maintenance system, is managed by a system of independent funds as the *Social Security* (Sozialversicherung). Historically there were established in 1883 the Health Insurance, in 1884 the Accident Insurance, in 1889 the Pension Insurance, in 1927 the Unemployment Insurance and in 1995 the Old Age Nursing Insurance.

Third, there is a strong emphasis on the principle of 'subsidiarity'. This principle is taken in Germany to mean both that services should be decentralised or independently managed, and that the level of state intervention should be residual -

[320] See for further details: Gesetz über die Mitbestimmung der Arbeitnehmer, Betriebsrätegesetz 1920 and Personalvertretungsgesetzen des Bundes und der Länder

[321] Officially: Grundgesetz für die Bundesrepublik Deutschland

[322] Officially: Verfassung des Deutschen Reiches

that is, limited to circumstances which are not adequately covered in other ways. Higher income earners are not covered by the main social insurance system, but are left to make their own arrangements.

The Social Market Economy (*Soziale Marktwirtschaft*) was originally promoted and implemented in West Germany by *Ludwig Erhard*, minister of economics and Alfred Müller-Armack, head of the policy department of the ministry of economics. under Chancellor *Konrad Adenauer* in 1949.

Konrad Adenauer with Ludwig Erhard (left to right) in 1956[323]

Therefore, the *Social Market Economy* as an extension of neo-liberal thought was not a defined economic order, but a holistic conception pursuing a complete humanistic societal order as a synthesis of seemingly conflicting objectives, namely economic freedom and social security. This socio-economic imperative actively managed by a strong state is often labelled by the ambiguous but historical term '*Der Dritte Weg*' (Third Way).[324] *Ludwig Erhard* pointed out that the principles of the *Social*

[323] http://en.wikipedia.org/wiki/Ludwig_Erhard
[324] http://en.wikipedia.org/wiki/Social_market_economy

Market Economy could only be achieved if the public was determined to give them priority.[325]

This presentation might be regarded as a pledge for an idealistic concept but contrary to this concept the *free market concept* is accepted for example in Australia. The present Australian Government and its public policies depend exclusively on the 'free' domestic and 'free' world market. Australia shows a strong dependence on money supply through national and international credit facilities. One may consider Australia as an underdeveloped country and in parts of it remains still a colony with very little national production, overwhelmingly engaged in services providing and exporting commodities.

Coming back to the non-representative survey *Questionnaire Private Household*[326], undertaken in late January 2013 til early February 2013, which might reflect a glimpse of a trend in *Western Societies,* the participants were asked "In times of economic downturn do you have the natural resources (e.g. vegetables & domestic animals) and the domestic ability to be self-sufficient?" Astonishingly 85.7% of the respondents said 'no'. They indicated the lack of a possibility to produce by themselves the necessary goods and services in their private household environment. Subsequently they depend on money and the various markets to 'survive' on a daily basis.

Q1. In times of economic downturn do you have the natural resources (e.g. vegetables & domestic animals) and the domestic ability to be self-sufficient?

	Response Percent	Response Count
Yes	11.7%	9
No	**85.7%**	**66**
N/A	2.6%	2
	answered question	**77**
	skipped question	**0**

[325] http://en.wikipedia.org/wiki/Social_market_economy
[326] See Appendix 4 Questionnaire Private Household

The following question "Do you agree that private households depend too much on money for obtaining goods and services?" confirmed the substantial dependency on the money supply of private households with the same 85.7% of the respondents answering with 'yes'.

Q2. Do you agree that private households depend too much on money for obtaining goods and services?

	Response Percent	Response Count
Yes	85.7%	66
No	13.0%	10
N/A	1.3%	1
answered question		77
skipped question		0

Q5. Which age group do you fall into?

	Response Percent	Response Count
15-19 years	1.3%	1
20-29 years	5.2%	4
30-39 years	19.5%	15
40-49 years	28.6%	22
50-59 years	24.7%	19
60-69 years	13.0%	10
70+ years	7.8%	6
answered question		77
skipped question		0

The outcome of this very limited small survey may be seen not only in a far-reaching reliance on the money supply but also on the embracing of 'money' as the *ultima ratio* of a human being's life. On the other hand there is much more to life than the pursuing of 'money' as some religions like the *Christianity* already have proposed. One might agree with *Anders Johansen* and *Didier Sornette,* who argued in their article '2050: The End of the Growth Era?' that "the evolution from a growth regime to a balanced symbiosis with nature and with the Earth's resources requires the transition to a knowledge based society, in which knowledge, intellectual, artistic and humanistic values replace the quest for material wealth."[327]

5.2 Aspects of Future Western Societies

There is only little doubt that the *private household production* has declined over the last century at least within *Western Societies.* In many of the basic three sections of private household production the *Industrialisation of private household production,* the *Mechanisation of private household production* and the *Centralisation of private household production* substantial changes have occurred, in particular to outsource former private household duties into the market and into governmental care. In all sections of private household production[328] where there is planning, such as nutrition, internal transport, storage, shopping, household cleaning, clothing, gardening and domestic animal care and personal care of household members, the alteration is obvious.

The issues of these days evolve into how the private household production will be embedded in future in *Western Societies* with their dominant free market concepts, even with various modifications? Is the Western civilization in decline? *Niall Ferguson* defines civilization as such: "Civilizations are partly a practical response by human populations to their environments – the challenges of feeding, watering, sheltering and defending themselves – but they are also cultural in character; often, though not always, religious; often, though not always, communities of language."[329] But is the future in a complex world relatively easy to determine? A comparison with astrophysics may be helpful to illustrate the dilemma of forecasting future significant events. *Paul Davies* wrote in his book 'The Mind of God – The Scientific Basis for a Rational World'[330]: "If the world is strictly deterministic, then all events are locked in a matrix of cause and effect. The past and future are contained in the

[327] Johansen & Sornette (2001)

[328] Fischer (1982), pp. 42-43.

[329] Ferguson (2011), p. xviii

[330] Davies (1992)

present, in the sense that the information needed to construct the past and future states of the world are folded into its present state just as rigidly as the information about Pythagoras' theorem is folded into the axioms of Euclidean geometry. The entire cosmos becomes a gigantic machine or clockwork, slavishly following a pathway of change already laid down from the beginning of time."[331] The opposite of determinism is indeterminism that is 'chance' or 'by accident' or by 'randomness', given something was not determined by something unspecified or unknown in regard of any object, event, action, situation or fact.

Paul Davies warned in his book 'The Eerie Silence – Are We Alone in the Universe?'[332] about the forthcoming potential dangers for humanity: "And of course it's not hard to identify potentially calamitous hazards that could wipe us all out – nuclear war, killer pandemics, comet impacts, social and economic disintegration ..."[333]. In line with this warning, apart from astrophysics, the British Astronomer *Sir Martin Rees*[334] provocatively raised up the disaster-proned query whether the 21st century would be the end of civilization.[335] *Sir Martin Rees* investigated more precisely the danger for the 21st Century in his book 'Our Final Hour – A Scientist's Warning: How Terror, Error, and Environmental Disaster Threaten Humankind's Future in This Century—On Earth and Beyond': "Science is advancing faster than ever, and on a broader front: bio-, cyber- and nanotechnology all offer exhilarating prospects; so does the exploration of space. But there is a dark side: new science can have unintended consequences; it empowers individuals to perpetrate acts of mega terror; even innocent errors could be catastrophic. The 'downside' from twenty-first century technology could be graver and more intractable than the threat of nuclear devastation that we have faced for decades. And human-induced pressures on the global environment may engender higher risks than the age-old hazards of earthquakes, eruptions, and asteroid impacts."[336] Furthermore The *Vatican* states: "We hear of aggression against life from conception to its natural end, the crisis of the family, and cultural and moral relativism. We hear of scientific and technological development that goes forward at all costs and in any direction possible, without giving a thought to ethics."[337] *Helmut Schmidt*, former Federal Chancellor of the Federal Republic of Germany (1973-1982), estimates the growth of the world population and the expansion of China within the world economy: "The growth of mankind after 2050 is difficult to estimate. Anyhow, many inhabitants will live in

---

331 Davies (1992), p. 29
332 Davies (2010)
333 ibid., p. 91
334 Baron Rees of Ludlow
335 Rees (2003)
336 ibid., p.vii
337 Zenit, The World seen from Rome, The Challenges of Today, 14th of December 2012, p.1

2050 and possibly China alone, as well as India, will then have a population equivalent to all the people who have existed on the whole world up to 1900".[338] [339] However, *Helmut Schmidt* qualifies the development of China as not so fast as other forecasters prefer. More moderately he comes up with the assessment "Also the average standard of living of the Chinese will still stay far behind. Large parts of China will still persevere long on the prosperity status of a developing country. At the same time, however, some provinces and cities of China will attain relatively quickly the scientific standards, the technological level and later also the economic capacity of Europe."[340]

On the other hand *Niall Ferguson* remains more optimistic about the survival of the Western Societies. In his book 'Civilization, The West and the Rest' he reasoned:[341] "My subsidiary question is this: if we can come up with a good explanation for the West's past ascendancy, can we then offer a prognosis for its future? Is this really the end of the West's world and the advent of a new Eastern epoch? Put differently, are we witnessing the waning of an age when the greater part of humanity was more or less subordinated to the civilization that arose in Western Europe in the wake of the Renaissance and Reformation – the civilization that, propelled by the Scientific Revolution and the Enlightenment, spread across the Atlantic and as far as the Antipodes, finally reaching its apogee during the Ages of Revolution, Industry and Empire?"[342] *Ferguson* is right by stating that the West "had patently enjoyed a real and sustained edge over the Rest for most of the previous 500 years."[343] On the contrary these are the centuries of *European Colonization*, and this happened often with military force or just by acclaiming the so called 'terra nullius'[344] for instance in the case of Australia.

The table below illustrates the situation of the territory, the population and the GDP of Western future empires 1500 AD with the situation of Western empires 1913 AD.

---

338 Schmidt, Helmut (2008) Außer Dienst – Eine Bilanz, Siedler Verlag München, p. 250

339 Translation by the author

340 Schmidt, Helmut (2008), p.252

341 Ferguson (2011)

342 ibid., pp. xv-xvi

343 ibid., p. 3

344 It is a Latin expression deriving from Roman law meaning "land belonging to no one", which is used in international law to describe territory which has never been subject to the sovereignty of any state, or over which any prior sovereign has expressly or implicitly relinquished sovereignty. http://en.wikipedia.org/wiki/Terra_nullius

Western Empires[345]

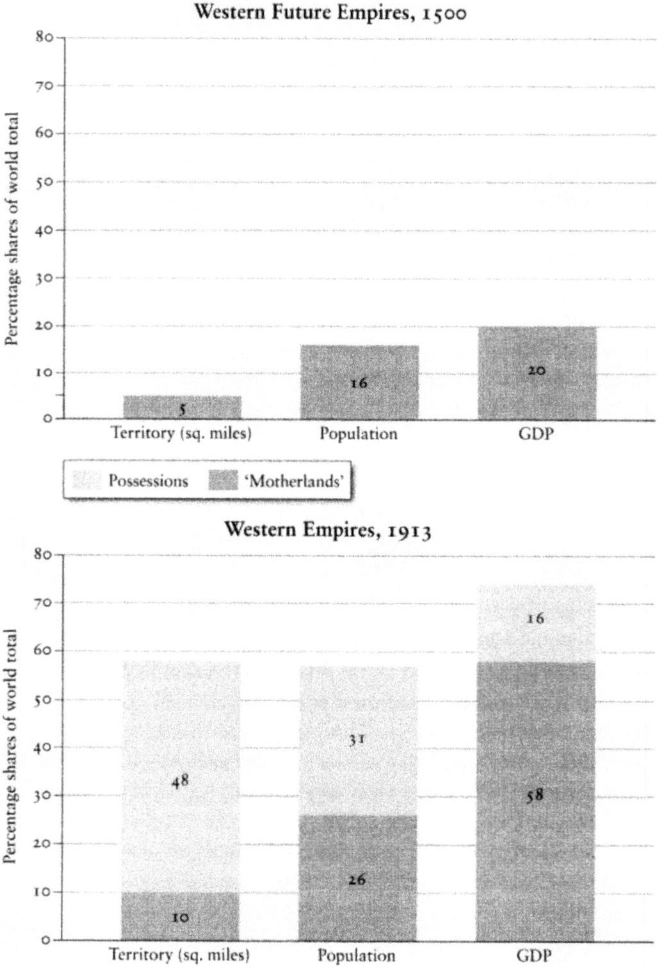

---

345 Based on data in Maddison, World Economy
The historic figures for global output (gross domestic product) must be treated with even more caution than those for population because of the heroic assumptions Maddison had to make to construct his estimates, and also because he elected to calculate GDP in terms of purchasing-power parity to allow for the much lower prices of non-traded goods in relatively poor countries.
Ferguson (2011), p. 7 & p. 326

These 'heroic' estimations and in particular the reconstruction of the data, which were certainly not available at the relevant time, might be for *Niall Ferguson* valuable in his arguments about the world dominance of the *Western Civilization* since 1500 AD, but these GDP quantities are quite questionable if not to a certain degree inadequate or at least in many ways arbitrary. Certainly the *European Colonization* has come to an end since the end of WWII through the independence of many formerly occupied territories. Nevertheless, the Western style consumerism has brought to the 'rest' of the world an ongoing temptation to copy the consumption patterns of Western Societies. *Ferguson* argues: "The result is one of the greatest paradoxes of modern history: that an economic system designed to offer infinite choice to the individual has ended up homogenizing humanity."[346] In conclusion of his analysis *Ferguson* has to offer a reverse of lacking courage: "Today, as then, the biggest threat to Western civilization is posed not by other civilizations but by our own pusillanimity – and by the historical ignorance that feeds it."[347]

Contrary to *Niall Ferguson*'s appeal and moral suasion in believing in the supreme values of Western Societies there are various proponents of the comparison of the downfall of the *Roman Empire* with the contemporary downfall of Western Societies. *Thomas Homer-Dixon* argues with optimism that *Western Societies* have the means to avoid a classical downfall like in the case of *Rome* and using the chances of a renewal of policies from a growth imperative to a resilience imperative.[348] "We have an advantage over the Romans that gives us a head start: we understand much better how the complex systems around us behave. It couldn't see clearly the multiple stresses converging on it; that it was bounded by the exigencies of its natural world; and that, as complexities and entrenched power accumulated, it was inexorably becoming a static, brittle system. We know that static, brittle systems don't survive. We also understand that in any complex adaptive system, breakdown, if limited, can be a key part of that system's long-term resilience and renewal. This knowledge - if we adopt the prospective mind that allows us to use if effectively - enables us to act with vastly greater wisdom than did the Romans."[349]

Celia Brayfield illustrates the 'downfall' in her book 'Deep France, A Writer's Year in the Béarn'[350] in the loss of the native culture in Great Britain: "American cultural imperialism and the demands of multiculturalism, our own native music has been almost obliterated, along with the communities which cherished it. Only a

---

[346] Ferguson (2011), p. 198
[347] ibid., p. 325
[348] Homer-Dixon (2008), p. 308
[349] ibid.
[350] Brayfield (2004)

micro-minority of musical anchorites are concerned to keep this despised heritage alive, and they get very little encouragement from sniffy civil servants, whose concern to promote 'diversity' has led to a suppression of our native culture. Ninety-five per cent of the English population probably couldn't sing one song that was known to their great-grandparents."[351] In response to the all embracing goal to acquire 'money' the Catholic Church is engaged in proposing that people rediscover the values of *Christianity*. While planned independently of each other, the *Year of Grace* is an initiative of the Australian Catholic Bishops in response to local issues, while the *Year of Faith* announced by *Pope Benedict XVI* is a call to the universal Church. Both have as their goal a renewal of faith in *Jesus Christ* in the face of a global secularism increasingly hostile to *Christian* belief and practice.[352] In Great Britain the public holiday Whit Monday was in 1967 abolished and replaced by the Spring Banking Holiday. How true this replacement relates to the highly adored goddess 'money'. Speaking to new ambassadors to the Vatican, *Pope Francis* said a major reason behind the increase in social and economic woes worldwide "is in our relationship with money and our acceptance of its power over ourselves and our society".[353] Furthermore "we have, he said, 'created new idols' where the 'golden calf of old' has found a new and heartless image in the cult of money and the dictatorship of an economy which is faceless and lacking any truly humane goal".[354] *Erik Reinert* criticized the search for 'money' in a more humoristic way: "Perhaps the best metaphor for today's economic situation in the West is that of Walt Disney's Uncle Scrooge and his bin of unproductive money (what the Bible refers to as 'mammon') representing a growing part of the financial sector. Scrooge's money is idle, and he only uses it for bathing purposes."[355]

Joseph Stiglitz former chief economist of the World Bank says that in the US equality of opportunity has been exposed as a myth. He warns: "An economic and political system that does not deliver for most citizens is one that is not sustainable in the long run. Eventually, faith in democracy and the market economy will erode, and the legitimacy of existing institutions and arrangements will be called into question."[356]

A recurrence to history with regard to predictions about the fate of *Western Societies* seems to be apt, for example, a comparison of *George Orwell's* 'Nineteen

---

351 Brayfield (2004), p. 263
352 Catholic Diocese of Townsville (2012) Contemplate the face of Christ 2012 to 2013
353 Rosengren (2013)
354 ibid.
355 Reinert (2012), p. 15
356 Byrne (2013)

Eighty-Four'[357] and *Aldous Huxley's* 'Brave New World'[358] and 'Brave New World Revisited'.[359] In 'Brave New World Revisited', *Aldous Huxley* concluded that the world was becoming like Brave New World much faster than he originally thought.

George Orwell (1903-1950)[360]

Aldous Leonard Huxley (1894-1963)[361]

"*Orwell* feared that the truth would be concealed from us. *Huxley* feared the truth would be drowned in a sea of irrelevance. *Orwell* feared we would become a captive culture. *Huxley* feared we would become a trivial culture, preoccupied with some equivalent of the feelies, the orgy porgy, and the centrifugal bumble puppy. As *Huxley* remarked in *Brave New World Revisited,* the civil libertarians and rationalists who are ever on the alert to oppose tyranny 'failed to take into account man's almost infinite appetite for distractions'. In 1984, *Orwell* added, people are controlled by inflicting pain. In *Brave New World,* they are controlled by inflicting pleasure. In short, *Orwell* feared that what we fear will ruin us. *Huxley* feared that our desire will ruin us."[362]

Christopher Hitchens, who himself published several articles on Huxley and a book on Orwell, noted the difference between the two texts. "We dwell in a present-tense culture that somehow, significantly, decided to employ the telling expression 'You're history' as a choice reprobation or insult, and thus elected to speak forgotten volumes about itself. By that standard, the forbidding dystopia of George *Orwell's*

[357] Dystopian novel by George Orwell published in 1949
[358] Novel written by Aldous Huxley and published in 1932
[359] Supplement to Brave New World written by Aldous Huxley and published 1958
[360] http://en.wikipedia.org/wiki/George_Orwell
[361] http://en.wikipedia.org/wiki/Aldous_Huxley
[362] http://en.wikipedia.org/wiki/Brave_New_World

Nineteen Eighty-Four already belongs, both as a text and as a date, with Ur and Mycenae, while the hedonist nihilism of *Huxley* still beckons toward a painless, amusement-sodden, and stress-free consensus. *Orwell's* was a house of horrors." [363] *Huxley* rightly argued in his book Brave New Word and Brave New World Revisited "In the field of mass communications as in almost every other field of enterprise, technological progress has hurt the Little Man and helped the Big Man. As lately as fifty years ago, every democratic country could boast of a great number of small journals and local newspapers. Thousands of country editors expressed thousands of independent opinions. Somewhere or other almost anybody could get almost anything printed. Today the press is still legally free; but most of the little papers have disappeared. The cost of wood-pulp, of modern printing machinery and of syndicated news is too high for the Little Man."[364] In a more compelling assurance he came to the declaration: "In their propaganda today's dictators rely for the most part on repetition, suppression and rationalization—the repetition of catchwords which they wish to be accepted as true, the suppression of facts which they wish to be ignored, the arousal and rationalization of passions which may be used in the interests of the Party or the State."[365] On the other hand *Huxley* propagated in 1958, against the current laws in Western Societies, more or less the use of drugs like LSD (lysergic acid diethylamide): "This extraordinary drug, which is effective in doses as small as fifty or even twenty-five millionths of a gram, has power (like peyote) to transport people into the other word. In the majority of cases, the other world to which LSD-25 gives access is heavenly; alternatively it may be purgatorial or even infernal. But, positive, or negative, the lysergic acid experience is felt by almost everyone who undergoes it to be profoundly significant and enlightening. In any event, the fact that minds can be changed so radically at so little cost to the body is altogether astonishing."[366]

Nevertheless *Huxley* might be right in his summary announcement about the state of affairs of the *Western Societies* "Our epoch has been given many nicknames - the Age of Anxiety, the Atomic Age, the Space Age. It might, with equally good reason, be called the Age of Television Addiction, the Age of Soap Opera, the Age of the Disk Jockey."[367]

In comparison of *Orwell's* and *Huxley's* prediction about the providence of *Humankind* one might summarize it in the mode that *Orwell* saw the people marching

---

363 Hitchens (1999), pp. 37–47
364 Huxley (1958), p. 266
365 ibid., p. 268
366 ibid., p. 300
367 ibid., p. 304

in doctrine of fascism, in uniforms and in military style in columns over the cliff whereas *Huxley* anticipated people dancing, with an idiotic smile, walking over the cliff. One might partially agree to *Huxley's* vision as much more appropriate for the destiny of *Western Societies*?

Recurring to the central theme about the development of private household production the question arises as to whether *Western Societies* will live through a forthcoming future of a 'downfall'.

Q4. Do you agree that Western societies and their focus on free markets, with individuals mostly pursuing money, will result in their downfall?[368]

	Response Percent	Response Count
Yes	60.5%	46
No	31.6%	24
N/A	7.9%	6
answered question		76
skipped question		1

Again mentioning the non-representative survey *Questionnaire Private Household*[369], undertaken in late January 2013 til early February 2013 a questionnaire was sent by the author as a web link provided by *SurveyMonkey*[370] [371] and via email, randomly distributed to roughly 1,000 interviewees. The non-representative results of the question 4 are quite surprising. A majority of 60.5% of respondents agreed that

368 See also Appendix 4

369 See Appendix 4 Questionnaire Private Household

370 SurveyMonkey is a web survey development cloud based (SaaS) company, founded in 1999 by Ryan Finley. The company acquired as a private limited until 2009, where it was sold to a private equity consortium. In 2010, the company received US$100 million in debt financing from Bank of America Merrill Lynch, and SunTrust Robinson Humphrey. SurveyMonkey has 185 employees, with offices in Palo Alto, California, Portland, Oregon, Seattle, Washington, Lisbon, São Paulo, and Luxembourg. It claims over 12 million registered customers.
See also: http://en.wikipedia.org/wiki/SurveyMonkey

371 BASIC account: the limits of a BASIC account are100 responses free.

Western Societies and their focus on free markets, with individuals mostly pursuing money, will result in their downfall. However, one has to take into account specific Australian conditions as an 'underdeveloped' country[372] depending on its export mostly of commodities and imports of many produced goods for private and commercial purpose. As an example might be taken that most overseas countries view their farmers and the food and fibre production as vital to their countries wellbeing, particularly as many countries have experienced chronic food shortages during the World Wars. Australians were spared that trauma and suffer the delusion that food security is not important and that we can simply import our needs. Presently Australia's food and fibre imports are rising faster than exports. Australia is now a net importer of fruit and veg, fish and pork.[373]

---

[372] This classification is not official but the author's assertion.
[373] Eagle, Neil (2013) Agriculture – Where to Now?

Conclusions

-------ꟾ------

Centuries ago the political economics was devoted to the development of private household production. Especially in the 19th century various scientists and 'revolutionaries' tried to work out a historical integration of the private household production into the economic division of labour as a development from the self-sufficient private household up to the modern economy with division of labour.

In particular at the beginning of the industrialization, and under the impression of that time and taking into account future possible social and economic transformations, there was established an unchallenged and widely held thesis that in the course of the industrial and social progress the private household production will be inevitably diminished, with some exemptions related to economic crises. Areas of the private household production with a much greater economic efficiency will be possibly integrated into the external private business and public sector.

In *Western Societies,* with their capitalist economic order, the private households have undergone substantial changes: The possibilities for private household production declined in various areas, for instance the raising up of children, caring for elderly people, food production and meal preparation, production of household durables, clothes etcetera. Further and further dependency of households on income and money supply to acquire articles or items for consumption arises.

The purpose of this research monograph was not looking for just a relatively short trend within the equipment of households with certain goods. The interest was to show the long term trend – compared to some graphs from the first sample survey of 1962 – of filling up the households with all the necessary 'production' means and now the trend to fill them up with communication means. It is inherent for a capitalistic free market to reduce the number of people living in households, in particular the percentage of single person and two person households, and to find some ways to produce goods and services in a wider range with the intention to gain profits for the relevant companies. In this way, the private households were deprived of their ability to produce essential goods and services by themselves, with no potential reassurance that in economic situations of retrogression or just 'mild' recession – notwithstanding the possibility to face a severe economic depression – with all the consequences in social and economic conditions for a meanwhile not existing society but a whole cluster of individualists. Or in terms of a social analysis: Australia for example has not yet achieved a national identity. The knowledge about household production in various divisions, for example the divisions of nutrition and clothes, has vanished over the last century substantially in probably all Western Societies. Or in other words: who had been trained by his grandmother how to scale a fish or just take the feathers off a chicken? The list can be expanded ad infinitum.

In the course of time it has been proven beyond doubt that the old fashioned (and related) concept of *Caveat Emptor* (sold as seen) has been denied for decades. It is indisputable that market failure relating to the lack of sufficient information about price, quality, durability, availability, time and environmental performance of consumer goods and services exists. It had been exposed that producers, not consumers are sovereign and that many of the wants being satisfied in *Western Economies* are nonurgent, even frivolous. The supply of money has become the *ultima ratio* for many private households, in particular those situated in cities and where people have to live in blocks of flats. There are little opportunities to extend the private household production, perhaps only on a small piece of land in allotments in the cities. Furthermore, those citizens who cannot take part in the *cash economy* or even in the *black market* most likely have to face the worst outcome of a depression.

Furthermore the concentration within the retail sector has taken away the so called 'corner shop' where the local food production was sold and sometimes they provided for people a place of socializing. One example may be the current *Hypermarkets,* which are superstores combining supermarkets and department stores, which mostly have become an anonymous 'shopping paradise' for those people who still have the money available to purchase the latest fashion or just the luxurious items of food.

Sometimes in *Western Societies* campaigns to support the national industry and agriculture through moral suasion directed to consumers like 'Buy Australian Made' or 'Buy American Apparel' or 'Shop Canadian' have been created as a form of import substitution. But overall, a consumer's responsibility is limited to think primarily of price, quality, durability, availability, time, environment, after sale service, and making a purchasing decision for their own benefit within these parameters. Consumers as individuals should not have an obligation to recognize within their purchasing decisions, what effect this will have for the national economy in the sense of a preferred demand for domestic products.

Private households and *cash economy* is another threat for the majority of private households, in particular for those private households which have virtually nothing to barter or even to be engaged in the cash economy. These private households have to spend their 'last' financial resources or even their 'valuables' in the cash economy to cope with the rough economic times. The lack of private household production is the penalty they have to suffer under.

Inflation is a further threat to private households depending on money supply. Inflation has an extensive notation within the *History of Economic Thought.* Once the inflation has reached a point of broader publicity that is when the overwhelming majority discover the substantial increase of the price level everywhere in the markets. Then the private households are caught in a severe misery and have to curtail their expenditures very drastically, if they are able to do so. The current economic situation in most of the Western Societies is quite different to the times for example with a 'house boom' or a 'mineral boom' and the majority of private households have lost the ability to countervail the inflation in the free markets and in the public service. In particular this matter can be detrimental once a high inflation or even a hyperinflation has taken place and then the misery of inflation can be identified as the cause of destruction of many private households and their members.

The main issue of self-sufficient private household production versus money dependency was how private households and their private household production are embedded in a well-rounded society. The starting point could be a preference and outline of the *social market concept* which may be deemed as one of the best orders of a society in modern ages. The post-war German resolution was based on the idea of a *social state*, sometimes portrayed as a *social market economy.* The *Social Market Economy* (*Soziale Marktwirtschaft*) is a form of market capitalism combined with a social policy favouring union bargaining and social insurance, and is sometimes classified as a coordinated market economy.

There is only little doubt that the *private household production* has declined over the last century at least within *Western Societies.* In many of the basic three sections of private household production the *Industrialisation of private household production,* the *Mechanisation of private household production* and the *Centralisation of private household production* substantial changes have occurred in particular to outsource former private household duties into the market and into governmental care. One might argue that this development has inevitably led to an irreversible process.

On the other hand a physicist like the British Astronomer Royal *Sir Martin Rees* warns us about our 'Final' experiment[374]. His concerns, which one might share, are related to the experiments in particle accelerators, especially at the Brookhaven National Laboratory in the United States of America and at CERN laboratory in Geneva in Switzerland, where eventually heavy atoms like gold and lead are used to crash by a speed close to the speed of light.[375] The result will be an enormous concentration of energy,[376] which could trigger theoretically damage to the fabric of space and therefore create a worst case scenario catastrophe, in which the entire earth just 'disappears' within an expanding bubble of empty space in the universe[377] . This scenario is most unlikely, but does humankind want to undertake for instance such experiments with a residual risk to play 'God'? These experiments are predominantly favoured in the Western style Societies.

Finally it has been questioned whether the *Western Societies* and their model of composing the lifestyle and their way of undertaking sciences to impose on other countries will survive – there are many pro and cons. This debate is just currently among eminent researchers worldwide. Sometimes one may ask himself whether *Aldous Huxley*'s thoughts published in his book '*Brave New World*'[378] will come partially true and furthermore symbolically described: "humankind will continue on a final path dancing with an idiotic smile on the face and falling over the cliff to extinguish itself". However *Leonard* argues in a more subtle manner: "This can seem all quaintly odd to us today because we seem to accept that our only convention is to flout convention. The done thing today is to undo what we've done before."[379] Furthermore perhaps *Nicolas Berdiaeff* [380] found a very veritable answer to the protagonist's of utopias:

---

[374] Rees (2003) p. 119
[375] ibid., p. 119
[376] ibid., p.120
[377] ibid., p. 121
[378] Huxley (1958)
[379] Leonard (2013), p. 1
[380] Nikolai Alexandrovich Berdyaev (Russian: иколай Алекса́ндрович Бердяев) (March 18, 1874 – March 24, 1948) was a Russian religious and political philosopher, who lived in exile in Paris. Huxley, Aldous (1958) Brave New World and Brave New World Revisited, Foreword by Christopher Hitchens, HarperCollins, New York, p. 1

Les utopies apparaissent comme bien plus réalisables qu'on ne le croyait autrefois. Et nous nous trouvons actuellement devant une question bien autrement angoissante: Comment éviter leur réalisation définitive? . . . Les utopies sont réalisables. La vie marche vers les utopies. Et peut-être un siècle nouveau commence-t-il, un siècle où les intellectuels et la classe cultivée rêveront aux moyens d'éviter les utopies et de retourner à une société non utopique, moins "parfaite" et plus libre.

—NICOLAS BERDIAEFF

Appendices

-------ഇ------

Appendix 1	The Green Thing
Appendix 2	Household projections by household type by region, 2006 to 2031, Australia
Appendix 3	Equipment of private household with staples in Germany 1998, 2003 & 2008
Appendix 4	Questionnaire Private Household Undertaken in January & February 2013
Appendix 5	Australian Bureau of Statistics Explanations to private household's statistic
Appendix 6	Australian Bureau of Statistics Merchandise Trades with the European Union (EU) 2009-2010

Appendix 1

The Green thing![381]

Checking out at the store, the young cashier suggested to the older woman that she should bring her own shopping bags because plastic bags weren't good for the environment. The woman apologized and explained, "We didn't have this green thing back in my earlier days."

The cashier responded, "That's our problem today. Your generation did not care enough to save our environment for future generations."

She was right -- our generation didn't have the green thing in its day. Back then, we returned milk bottles, pop bottles and beer bottles to the store. The store sent them back to the plant to be washed and sterilized and refilled, so it could use the same bottles over and over. So they really were recycled. We refilled writing pens with ink instead of buying a new pen, and we replaced the razor blades in a razor instead of throwing away the whole razor just because the blade got dull.

But we didn't have the green thing back in our day.

We walked up stairs, because we didn't have an escalator in every shop and office building. We walked to the grocery store and didn't climb into a 300-horsepower machine every time we had to go two blocks.

But she was right. We didn't have the green thing in our day.

Back then, we washed the baby's nappies because we didn't have the throw-away kind. We dried clothes on a line, not in an energy gobbling machine burning up 220 volts -- wind and solar power really did dry our clothes back in our early days. Kids got hand-me-down clothes from their brothers or sisters, not always brand-new clothing.

But that young lady is right. We didn't have the green thing back in our day.

Back then, we had one TV, or radio, in the house -- not a TV in every room. And the TV had a small screen the size of a handkerchief (remember them?), not a

[381] Unknown source

screen the size of the county of Yorkshire. In the kitchen, we blended and stirred by hand because we didn't have electric machines to do everything for us. When we packaged a fragile item to send in the post, we used wadded up old newspapers to cushion it, not Styrofoam or plastic bubble wrap. Back then, we didn't fire up an engine and burn petrol just to cut the lawn. We used a push mower that ran on human power. We exercised by working so we didn't need to go to a health club to run on treadmills that operate on electricity.

But she's right. We didn't have the green thing back then.

We drank water from a fountain or a tap when we were thirsty instead of demanding a plastic bottle flown in from another country. We accepted that a lot of food was seasonal and didn't expect that to be bucked by flying it thousands of air miles around the world. We actually cooked food that didn't come out of a packet, tin or plastic wrap and we could even wash our own vegetables and chop our own salad.

But we didn't have the green thing back then.

Back then, people took the tram or a bus, and kids rode their bikes to school or walked instead of turning their mothers into a 24-hour taxi service. We had one electrical outlet in a room, not an entire bank of sockets to power a dozen appliances. And we didn't need a computerized gadget to receive a signal beamed from satellites 2,000 miles out in space in order to find the nearest pizza joint.

But isn't it sad the current generation laments how wasteful we old folks were just because we didn't have the green thing back then?

Appendix 2

Household projections by household type by region, 2006 to 2031, Australia[382]

Statistical division	Household type	Year					
		2006	2011	2016	2021	2026	2031
		— '000 —					
Brisbane	Couple family with children households	217.8	229.6	243.0	256.6	270.9	283.5
	Couple without children households	175.4	204.1	238.8	270.3	296.7	321.0
	One-parent family households	78.3	90.7	100.8	109.4	117.3	125.2
	Other family households	10.3	11.0	11.9	12.5	13.2	13.9
	Group households	31.8	33.6	36.1	38.0	39.7	41.8
	Lone-person households	153.6	175.7	202.1	230.0	256.9	283.8
	Not classifiable	26.4	28.8	31.5	33.9	36.1	38.1
	Total	*693.5*	*773.5*	*864.1*	*950.6*	*1,030.7*	*1,107.3*
Gold Coast	Couple family with children households	56.1	63.6	71.1	77.9	83.7	88.6
	Couple without children households	57.0	67.0	78.6	89.5	99.2	108.2
	One-parent family households	23.6	28.8	33.3	37.2	40.3	43.3
	Other family households	2.2	2.6	2.9	3.1	3.4	3.6
	Group households	10.4	11.2	12.2	12.9	13.8	14.7
	Lone-person households	46.7	55.6	65.1	74.6	83.8	92.5
	Not classifiable	14.4	16.6	18.8	20.8	22.5	24.1
	Total	*210.3*	*245.3*	*282.0*	*316.1*	*346.6*	*375.0*
Sunshine Coast	Couple family with children households	32.1	35.7	39.2	42.5	45.9	49.2
	Couple without children households	37.4	43.7	50.3	57.0	63.3	69.7
	One-parent family households	13.4	16.0	18.0	19.8	21.5	23.3
	Other family households	0.9	1.1	1.2	1.3	1.4	1.5
	Group households	4.2	4.7	5.1	5.4	5.8	6.3
	Lone-person households	27.2	31.9	36.7	41.7	46.9	52.5

382 Queensland State and Regional Household and Dwelling Projections 2006 to 2031 (2008 release), Queensland Centre for Population Research, University of Queensland

Statistical division	Household type	Year					
		2006	2011	2016	2021	2026	2031
				— '000 —			
	Not classifiable	5.0	5.7	6.4	7.0	7.6	8.2
	Total	*120.2*	*138.7*	*157.0*	*174.7*	*192.4*	*210.6*
West Moreton	Couple family with children households	8.5	8.9	9.7	10.7	11.8	12.8
	Couple without children households	8.5	10.4	12.4	14.3	16.1	17.9
	One-parent family households	2.9	3.6	4.3	4.9	5.5	6.0
	Other family households	0.3	0.3	0.3	0.4	0.4	0.4
	Group households	0.7	0.7	0.8	0.9	1.0	1.1
	Lone-person households	5.7	6.6	7.6	8.9	10.2	11.7
	Not classifiable	0.9	1.0	1.1	1.2	1.4	1.5
	Total	*27.4*	*31.5*	*36.3*	*41.4*	*46.4*	*51.5*
Wide Bay-Burnett	Couple family with children households	28.3	29.0	29.8	30.9	32.7	34.6
	Couple without children households	35.6	42.1	47.7	52.7	57.4	62.1
	One-parent family households	12.2	15.0	16.8	18.2	19.5	20.8
	Other family households	0.8	0.9	0.9	1.0	1.0	1.1
	Group households	2.8	3.4	3.7	4.0	4.2	4.5
	Lone-person households	25.8	30.4	34.6	38.6	42.7	47.2
	Not classifiable	3.1	3.5	3.7	4.0	4.3	4.6
	Total	*108.8*	*124.2*	*137.4*	*149.4*	*161.8*	*174.9*
Darling Downs	Couple family with children households	26.5	26.8	27.7	29.0	30.5	31.8
	Couple without children households	25.2	29.7	33.9	37.8	41.1	44.3
	One-parent family households	9.0	10.2	11.1	12.0	12.7	13.5
	Other family households	1.0	1.1	1.2	1.2	1.3	1.4
	Group households	2.6	2.6	2.7	2.8	2.9	3.1
	Lone-person households	21.3	24.6	27.9	31.3	34.6	38.1
	Not classifiable	2.3	2.5	2.6	2.8	3.0	3.1
	Total	*87.9*	*97.5*	*107.1*	*117.0*	*126.1*	*135.3*
South West	Couple family with children households	3.2	3.0	2.9	3.0	3.0	3.0
	Couple without children households	2.8	3.1	3.3	3.5	3.5	3.6
	One-parent family	1.0	1.0	1.0	1.0	1.0	1.0

Statistical division	Household type	Year					
		2006	2011	2016	2021	2026	2031
				— '000 —			
	households						
	Other family households	0.1	0.1	0.1	0.1	0.1	0.1
	Group households	0.3	0.3	0.3	0.3	0.3	0.3
	Lone-person households	2.8	2.8	3.0	3.2	3.3	3.4
	Not classifiable	0.3	0.3	0.3	0.3	0.3	0.3
	Total	*10.5*	*10.6*	*11.0*	*11.4*	*11.6*	*11.8*
Fitzroy	Couple family with children households	24.3	25.7	26.9	28.4	30.3	32.1
	Couple without children households	20.4	24.7	28.3	31.5	34.5	37.5
	One-parent family households	8.0	9.4	10.4	11.3	12.1	13.0
	Other family households	0.8	0.8	0.8	0.9	0.9	1.0
	Group households	2.2	2.3	2.4	2.4	2.6	2.7
	Lone-person households	16.9	20.4	23.3	26.2	29.1	32.2
	Not classifiable	3.0	3.4	3.7	3.9	4.2	4.5
	Total	*75.7*	*86.7*	*95.8*	*104.6*	*113.8*	*122.9*
Central West	Couple family with children households	1.4	1.2	1.2	1.2	1.3	1.3
	Couple without children households	1.3	1.3	1.4	1.5	1.6	1.6
	One-parent family households	0.4	0.4	0.5	0.5	0.5	0.5
	Other family households	0.1	0.1	0.1	0.1	0.1	0.1
	Group households	0.1	0.1	0.1	0.1	0.1	0.1
	Lone-person households	1.4	1.4	1.5	1.5	1.6	1.7
	Not classifiable	0.2	0.2	0.2	0.2	0.2	0.2
	Total	*4.8*	*4.8*	*5.0*	*5.1*	*5.3*	*5.5*
Mackay	Couple family with children households	19.6	21.7	24.1	26.0	27.2	27.9
	Couple without children households	16.5	20.4	24.2	27.2	29.2	31.1
	One-parent family households	5.4	6.3	7.3	7.9	8.5	8.9
	Other family households	0.5	0.6	0.7	0.7	0.7	0.8
	Group households	1.9	2.1	2.3	2.4	2.5	2.6
	Lone-person households	12.3	14.8	17.5	19.9	21.8	23.7
	Not classifiable	3.9	4.5	5.2	5.6	6.0	6.2
	Total	*60.1*	*70.4*	*81.1*	*89.8*	*95.9*	*101.1*

Statistical division	Household type	Year					
		2006	2011	2016	2021	2026	2031
		— '000 —					
Northern	Couple family with children households	24.1	25.6	27.4	28.6	29.7	30.5
	Couple without children households	20.9	25.0	29.8	34.0	37.1	39.9
	One-parent family households	9.1	10.9	12.2	13.2	13.9	14.5
	Other family households	1.0	1.1	1.3	1.3	1.4	1.4
	Group households	3.2	3.5	3.8	4.0	4.1	4.2
	Lone-person households	17.7	21.6	25.9	29.6	32.9	36.0
	Not classifiable	3.1	3.5	3.9	4.2	4.5	4.7
	Total	*79.1*	*91.1*	*104.3*	*115.0*	*123.6*	*131.4*
Far North	Couple family with children households	26.0	26.5	26.8	27.4	28.5	29.7
	Couple without children households	24.4	29.5	33.8	37.5	40.5	43.2
	One-parent family households	11.6	13.4	14.5	15.3	16.1	17.0
	Other family households	1.1	1.3	1.4	1.4	1.5	1.6
	Group households	3.6	3.3	3.2	3.1	3.3	3.5
	Lone-person households	23.0	28.1	32.3	36.3	39.9	43.6
	Not classifiable	6.3	6.9	7.3	7.7	8.0	8.5
	Total	*95.9*	*108.9*	*119.3*	*128.7*	*137.7*	*147.0*
North West	Couple family with children households	3.5	3.5	3.2	3.1	3.1	3.2
	Couple without children households	2.6	3.5	3.8	4.0	4.2	4.3
	One-parent family households	1.3	1.4	1.3	1.3	1.3	1.4
	Other family households	0.1	0.1	0.1	0.1	0.1	0.1
	Group households	0.4	0.4	0.4	0.3	0.3	0.3
	Lone-person households	2.7	3.2	3.4	3.6	3.8	4.1
	Not classifiable	1.1	1.2	1.2	1.2	1.2	1.2
	Total	*11.8*	*13.5*	*13.4*	*13.7*	*14.1*	*14.6*
Queensland	Couple family with children households	471.3	500.8	533.1	565.3	598.6	628.1
	Couple without children households	428.0	504.5	586.5	660.9	724.3	784.4
	One-parent family households	176.0	206.9	231.4	252.0	270.1	288.4
	Other family	19.2	21.2	23.0	24.2	25.6	27.1

Statistical division	Household type	Year					
		2006	**2011**	**2016**	**2021**	**2026**	**2031**
				— '000 —			
	households						
	Group households	64.3	68.3	73.0	76.7	80.7	85.3
	Lone-person households	357.1	416.9	480.9	545.5	607.6	670.5
	Not classifiable	70.0	78.0	85.8	92.8	99.1	105.3
	Total	**1,585.9**	**1,796.6**	**2,013.7**	**2,217.4**	**2,406.0**	**2,589.1**

Appendix 3

Equipment of private households with staples in Germany 1998, 2003 & 2008[383]

Equipment of private households with staples in Germany
Equipment Rate

Items	Germany		
	1998	2003	2008
Households covered (Number)	68 863	59 713	58 984
Households projected (1,000)	36 703	37 931	39 077
	Equipment Rate Equipment per 100 Household in %		
Vehicles			
Motor car	*75.1*	*76.9*	*77.1*
new	*37.0*	*35.0*	*31.3*
second hand	*43.8*	*47.4*	*50.3*
leased1	*2.3*	*3.4*	*4.3*
Motor cycle (incl. scooter)	*10.9*	*11.6*	*11.6*
Bicycle	*80.0*	*78.6*	*79.5*
Media Staples			
Television	*95.8*	*94.4*	*94.1*
incl. flat-screen television	.	.	*15.7*
Satellite reception equipment	*28.8*	*36.8*	*39.1*
Cable TV connection	*53.4*	*52.6*	*47.8*
DVB-T-decoder	.	.	*16.2*
Pay-TV-decoder	.	.	*4.7*
DVD player (for TV or on PC)	.	*27.1*	*69.1*
Camcorder (video camera)	*16.6*	*21.9*	*19.5*
Camcorder (video camera), analogue	.	*17.3*	*11.1*
Camcorder (video camera), digital	.	*7.0*	*9.7*
Photo camera	*86.3*	*83.4*	*85.2*
Photo camera, analogue	.	.	*61.4*
Photo camera, digital	.	.	*58.3*
MP3-player	.	.	*37.3*
CD player/recorder	.	.	*79.7*
Gaming console	.	.	*19.4*

383 Statistisches Bundesamt (2007) Wirtschaftsrechnungen, Einkommens- und Verbrauchs-stichprobe 2008, Ausstattung privater Haushalte mit ausgewählten Gebrauchsgütern, Fachserie 15, Heft 1, Wiesbaden

Information Staples			
Personal computer	38.7	61.4	75.4
PC, fixed	.	58.2	62.1
PC, mobile (notebook, laptop, netbook)	.	10.7	34.7
Internet connection or access	8.1	46.0	64.4
ISDN-connection	5.6	23.4	31.5
Telephone	.	98.7	99.0
Telephone, fixed	96.8	94.5	89.7
Telephone, mobile	11.2	72.5	86.3
Telephone answering machine, fixed	36.8	46.2	49.4
Fax machine, fixed	14.8	20.7	20.7
Car navigation system	.	.	20.7
Household Appliances			
Refrigerator (also with freezer compartment)	99.0	98.8	98.6
Freezer	77.4	66.0	52.4
Dishwasher	44.8	56.6	62.5
Micro-wave oven	50.8	62.7	69.6
Dryer	29.4	36.5	38.5
Hometrainer	.	24.3	27.5

Appendix 4

Questionnaire Private Household
Undertaken in January & February 2013

Dear Consumer

The accompanying survey is part of a research project "Private Household and Money Supply – A Law and Economics Approach" being conducted by Professor Dr.rer.pol. Wolfgang Chr. Fischer, Emeritus Professor of Economics, University of Bremen, Germany.

The aim of the survey is to determine the development of private household production & services and associated factors for maintaining a buffer function in times of economic downturn. Often this crucial issue had been regarded in the relevant literature of Law and Economics as a quantité négligeable.

As I realise that your time is valuable the survey will hopefully take a minimum time to answer. All the five questions can be answered by simply ticking the most appropriate response. All replies are strictly confidential and anonymous.

If you have any questions please feel free to contact me on email: wolfgang.fischer@uni-bremen.de.

Thank you for taking the time to complete the survey.

Professor Dr. Wolfgang Chr. Fischer
Magnetic Island QLD 4819, South Pacific, Australia

Q1 Edit Question ▼ Add Question Logic Move Copy Delete

1. In times of economic downturn do you have the natural resources (e.g. vegetables & domestic animals) and the domestic ability to be self-sufficient?

○ Yes

○ No

○ N/A

Q2 Edit Question ▼ Add Question Logic Move Copy Delete

2. Do you agree that private households depend too much on money for obtaining goods and services?

○ Yes

○ No

○ N/A

Q3 Edit Question ▼ Add Question Logic Move Copy Delete

3. Should domestic science be a compulsory subject in primary schools for a period of more than two years?

- ◯ Yes
- ◯ No
- ◯ N/A

Q4 Edit Question ▼ Add Question Logic Move Copy Delete

4. Do you agree that Western societies and their focus on free markets, with individuals mostly pursuing money, will result in their downfall?

- ◯ Yes
- ◯ No
- ◯ N/A

Q5 Edit Question ▼ Add Question Logic Move Copy Delete

5. Which age group do you fall into?

- ◯ 15-19 years
- ◯ 20-29 years
- ◯ 30-39 years
- ◯ 40-49 years
- ◯ 50-59 years
- ◯ 60-69 years
- ◯ 70+ years

Appendix 5

Australian Bureau of Statistics
Explanations to private household's statistic[384]

Average household size
Average household size refers to the number of persons per household in private dwellings.

Child
A child is a person of any age who is a natural, adopted, step or foster son or daughter of a couple or lone parent, usually resident in the same household. A child is also any individual under 15 years, usually resident in the household, who forms a parent-child relationship with another member of the household. This includes otherwise related children under 15 years and unrelated children under 15 years.

In order to be classified as a child, the persons can have no partner or child of his/her own usually resident in the household. A separate family in the household is formed in this instance. If a person is aged under 15 years and has a partner/spouse these relationships are not recorded.

Couple family with children
A family based on two persons who are in a registered or de facto marriage, who are usually resident in the same household. The family must include one or more children usually resident in the same household. The family may include any number of other related individuals usually resident in the household.

Couple family without children
A family based on two persons who are in a registered or de facto marriage, who are usually resident in the same household and have no children usually resident in the same household. The family may include any number of other related individuals usually resident in the household.

Family
A family is defined by the ABS as two or more persons, one of whom is at least 15 years of age, who are related by blood, marriage (registered or de facto), adoption, step or fostering, and who are usually resident in the same household. The basis of a family is formed by identifying the presence of either a couple relationship, lone

384 ABS 3236.0 - Household and Family Projections, Australia, 2006 to 2031

parent-child relationship or other blood relationship. Some households will contain more than one family.

Group household

A group household is a household consisting of two or more unrelated people where all persons are aged 15 years or over. There are no reported couple relationships, parent-child relationships or other blood relationships in these households.

Household

A household is a group of two or more related or unrelated people who usually reside in the same dwelling who regard themselves as a household and who make common provision for food or other essentials for living; or a person living in a dwelling who makes provision for his or her own food and other essentials for living, without combining with any other person. Households include group households of unrelated persons, same-sex couple households, single-parent households as well as one-person households.

A household usually resides in a private dwelling (including caravans etc. in caravan parks). Persons usually resident in non-private dwellings, such as hotels, motels, boarding houses, gaols and hospitals, are not included in household estimates.

A household is defined as one or more persons, at least one of whom is at least 15 years of age, usually resident in the same private dwelling. The Census categorises households as discrete units, thus the projection method is based on the assumption that households are discrete units. It is acknowledged that some living arrangements are fluid and that because of study, work or shared care arrangements, a family member may be associated with more than one household. For example, full-time students living away from home may still be dependent on their family household.

Appendix 6

Australian Bureau of Statistics
Australia's Merchandise Trades with the European Union (EU) (a)
2009 -2010[385]

	Value ($A million)		Share of total (%)	% Change
	2009	2010	2010	2009
Top 20 merchandise exports				
Gold	5,606	5,222	28.1	-6.9
Coal	2,498	3,934	21.2	57.5
Alcoholic beverages	957	817	4.4	-14.6
Other ores & concentrates (b)	202	615	3.3	204.1
Medicaments (incl veterinary)	644	426	2.3	-33.8
Lead	365	405	2.2	10.8
Gold coin & legal tender coin	355	366	2.0	3.0
Misc manufactured articles, nes	201	234	1.3	16.3
Wool & other animal hair (incl tops)	135	226	1.2	67.1
Precious metal ores & conc (excl gold)	41	216	1.2	426.4
Non-ferrous waste & scrap	147	178	1.0	20.9
Measuring & analysing instruments	175	177	1.0	1.3
Aircraft, spacecraft & parts	212	172	0.9	-18.9
Oil-seeds & oleaginous fruits, soft	405	170	0.9	-58.0
Medical instruments (incl veterinary)	249	158	0.9	-36.5
Nickel (c)	59	152	0.8	158.2
Meat (excl beef), f.c.f.	160	143	0.8	-10.7
Iron ore & concentrates	38	141	0.8	267.8
Telecom equipment & parts	87	118	0.6	35.3
Electrical circuits equipment	119	109	0.6	-8.7
Total commodities	17,400	18,567	100.0	6.7

385 Delegation of the European Union to Australia (2011) EU-Australia Economic Relationship, Canberra, p.9, Source: DFAT, personal communication (3 August 2011)

	Value ($A million)		Share of total (%)	% Change
	2009	2010	2010	2009
Top 20 merchandise imports (d)				
Medicaments (incl veterinary)	5,258	5,355	13.9	1.9
Passenger motor vehicles	2,851	3,906	10.2	37.0
Organo-inorganic compounds	1,146	1,131	2.9	-1.2
Civil engineering equipment & parts	777	921	2.4	18.5
Measuring & analysing instruments	948	903	2.4	-4.7
Pharm products (excl medicaments)	858	881	2.3	2.7
Vehicle parts & accessories	659	744	1.9	12.8
Telecom equipment & parts	842	728	1.9	-13.5
Specialised machinery & parts	955	696	1.8	-27.1
Goods vehicles	481	645	1.7	34.1
Alcoholic beverages	598	608	1.6	1.8
Mechanical handling equip & parts	775	600	1.6	-22.5
Edible products & preparations, nes	721	589	1.5	-18.4
Pumps (excl liquid pumps) & parts	790	587	1.5	-25.7
Medical instruments (incl veterinary)	567	551	1.4	-2.9
Electrical circuits equipment	534	529	1.4	-0.9
Perfumery & cosmetics (excl soap)	524	520	1.4	-0.7
Misc manufactured articles, nes	497	516	1.3	3.9
Paper & paperboard	571	500	1.3	-12.5
Railway vehicles (incl hovertrains)	329	454	1.2	37.9
Total commodities	39,483	38,417	100.0	-2.7

(a) Rank based on 2010.

(b) Mainly Zinc ores & concentrates and Lead ores & concentrates.

(c) Excludes Nickel mattes, Nickel oxide sinters and Nickel unwrought. Refer to Table A in the analysis.

(d) Imports of aircraft were made confidential by the ABS from Sep-08 onwards and are excluded from total imports.

References

-------ꝏ------

Adolph, Robert (1919) Einküchenwirtschaft als soziale Aufgabe, Berlin, Germany.

Anderson, Benjamin (1930) Chief Economist of Chase National Bank, New York Times, April.

Australian Bureau of Statistics (2010), 32360DO001_20062031 Household and Family Projections, Australia, 2006 to 2031, Canberra, Australia.

Australian Bureau of Statistics (2010) 3236.0 - Household and Family Projections, Australia, 2006 to 2031, Canberra, Australia.

Australian Bureau of Statistics (2007) Census 2006, No: 20630-qm29-Australia (Australia).

Australian Bureau of Statistics (2002) Catalogue No. 8622.0, 10, Canberra, Australia.

Australian Consumers' Association (1993) Should you Buy Australian?, Choice, January 1993, Marrickville NSW, Australia.

Bainbridge, Lister & Jones, Peter (1992) The Politics of Tolerance: The Use of Gendered Self in Social Welfare Education and Practice, Paper presented at the Annual National Conference of the Australian Association for Social Work and Welfare Education, Sydney, Australia.

Baranger, Michel (2008) Chaos, Complexity, and Entropy – A physics talk for non-physicists, Massachusetts Institute of Technology, Center for Theoretical Physics, No. 3112.

Bebel, August (1922) Die Frau und der Sozialismus, 50. Auflage, Stuttgart und Berlin, Germany.

Bichler, Shimshon and Nitzan, Jonathan (2012) Capital as power: Toward a new cosmology of capitalism, in: real-world economics review, issue no. 61.

Bielfeld, Gretha (1930) Die Mechanisierung des Haushalts und ihre volkswirtschaftliche Bedeutung, in: Veröffentlichung des Instituts für Hauswirtschaftswissenschaft an der Akademie für soziale und pädagogische Frauenarbeit in Berlin, Heft 6, Langensalza, Germany.

Black, Terry (1995) Buy Australian? Myths and Realities, Centre for Independent Studies, Policy Monograph 30, St Leonards NSW, Australia.

Braun, Lilly (1901) Frauenarbeit und Hauswirtschaft, Berlin, Germany.

Brayfield, Celia (2004) Deep France, A Writer's Year in the Béarn, Pan Books, London, Great Britain.
Brecht, Bertolt (1962) Die heilige Johanna der Schlachthöfe (Saint Joan of the Stockyards), edition suhrkamp 1st edition, Berlin, Germany.
Brunetta, Renato & Ceci, Anna (1998) Underground employment in Italy: its causes, its extent and the costs and benefits of regularization, in: Review of economic conditions in Italy, No. 2.
Brunner, Otto (1956) Hausvaeterliteratur, in: Handwoerterbuch der Sozial-wissenschaften, 5. Band, Göttingen, Germany.
Brunner, Otto (1952) Die alteuropäsche "Ökonomik", in: Zeitschrift für National-ökonomie, Bd. 13, Wien, Austria.
Bryan, Michael F. (1997) 'On the Origin and Evolution of the Word Inflation', Economic Commentary Federal Reserve Bank of Cleveland, October 15.
Bücher, Karl (1917) Die Entstehung der Volkswirtschaft, Erste Sammlung, 10. Aufl., Tübingen, Germany.
Butler, David (1998) Chair, Cash Economy Task Force, Commissioner of Taxation, Improving Tax Compliance in the Cash Economy, Canberra, Australia.
Byrne, Patrick (2013) News Weekly No. 2894, March 2.
Caragata, Patrick J. & Giles, David E.A. (1998) Simulating the Relationship Between the Hidden Economy and the Tax Level and Tax Mix in New Zealand.
Catholic Diocese of Townsville (2012) Contemplate the face of Christ 2012 to 2013.
Clark, Manning (1992) A Short History of Australia, 2nd Edition, Ringwood, Victoria, Australia.
Coltheart, Lenore (editor) (2004) Jessie Street, A revised autobiography, The Federation Press, Sydney, Australia.
Complexity Economics (2010) http://en.wikipedia.org/wiki/Complexity_economics.
Davies, Paul (2010) The Eerie Silence – Are We Alone in the Universe? Penguin Books, London, England.
Davies, Paul (1994) The Last Three Minutes, Basic Books, New York, USA.
Davies, Paul (1992) The Mind of God – The Scientific Basis for a Rational World, Simon & Schuster, New York, USA.
Davies, Paul (1987) The Cosmic Blueprint, Heinemann, London, Great Britain.
Delegation of the European Union to Australia (2011), EU-Australia Economic Relationship, Canberra, Australia.
Devonshire, Deborah (2010) Wait For Me! Memoirs of the Youngest Mitford Sister, John Murray, London, Great Britain.
Egner, Erich (1967) Zum Verständnis des hauswirtschaftlichen Sturkturwandels, in: Beiträge zur Ökonomie von Haushalt und Verbrauch, Heft 3, Berlin, Germany.

Egner, Erich (1964) Die volkswirtschaftliche Funktion der Familienhaushalte, in: Jahrbuch für Sozialwissenschaft, Bd. 15, Göttingen, Germany.

Egner, Erich (1958) Eigenart und Aufgabe hauswirtschaftlicher Forschung, in: Zeitschrift für die gesamte Staatswissenschaft, 114. Band, Tübingen, Germany.

Egner, Erich (1956) Haushalt, in: Handwörterbuch der Sozialwissenschaften, 5. Band, Göttingen, Germany.

Egner, Erich (1953) Die Rolle des Haushalts in der Geistesgeschichte, in: Hauswirtschaft und Wissenschaft, Jg. 1, Heft 1, Hamburg, Germany.

Egner, Erich (1952) Der Haushalt, Eine Darstellung seiner volkswirtschaftlichen Gestalt, Berlin, Germany.

Engels, Friedrich (1962) Der Ursprung der Familie, des Privateigentums und des Staates, in: Karl Marx/Friedrich Engels Werke, Band 21, Berlin, Germany. This Treatise was published for the first time at Zürich in 1884.

Essig, Olga (1920) Der hauswirtschaftliche Groβbetrieb; Eine wirtschaftswissenschaftliche Studie; Frankfurt, Germany.

European Commission (1999) Consumer Policy Action Plan 1999-2001, http://europa.eu.int/commm/dg24, Brussels, Belgium.

European Commission (1998) Directorate General XXI, Division Customs and Indirect Taxation, XXI/900/98-EN, Brussels, Belgium.

Ferguson, Niall (2011) Civilization – The West and the Rest, Penguin Press, New York, USA.

Ferguson, Niall (2010) Complexity and Collapse – Empire on the Edge of Chaos, Foreign Affairs, Vol. 89, No. 2, New York.

Fexman, Bruce (1997) Canadian Attitudes Towards Taxation, in: The Underground Economy: Global Evidence of its Size and Impact, in: Global Evidence of its Size and Impact, Section 1, The Fraser Institute Vancouver, BC, Canada.

Fischer Wolfgang Chr. (2010) German Hyperinflation 1922/23 – A Law and Economics Approach, Eul Verlag, Köln, Germany.

Fischer, Wolfgang Chr. (1990) Zentralisierung der Hauswirtschaft - eine Alternative zur traditionellen Aufgabenverteilung im privaten Haushalt? In: Zeitschrift Erwägen Wissen Ethik (EWE) vormals: Ethik und Sozialwissenschaften (EuS) zu Genderthemen, EuS-Heft 2, Jg. 1, Paderborn, Germany.

Fischer, Wolfgang Chr. (1984) Eine geteilte Gesellschaft - Implikationen für die Verbraucherpolitik in westlichen Industriestaaten, Hauswirtschaftliche Bildung, No. 2, Baltmannsweiler, Germany.

Fischer, Wolfgang Chr. (1982) Entwicklung der privaten Hauswirtschaft, Burgbücherei, Baltmannsweiler, Germany.

Fischer, Wolfgang Chr. (1978) Aspekte der Einfluβnahme privater Haushalte auf die Kollektivgüterversorgung, in: Hauswirtschaft und Wissenschaft, Heft 3, München, Germany.

Fischer, Wolfgang Chr. (1972) Sozial-Ökonomische Aspekte der Entwicklung der Privaten Hauswirtschaft, Inaugural-Dissertation, Rechts- und Staatswissenschaftliche Fakultät der Rheinischen Friedrich-Wilhelms-Universität zu Bonn, Universitäts Druckerei Bonn, Germany.

Fischer, Wolfgang Chr. & Byron, Peter (1995) Buy Australian Made, Department of Economics, Research Monograph, James Cook University, Townsville, Australia.

Fischer, Wolfgang Chr. & Byron, Peter & Lehnert, Günter (1999) Federal Consumption Tax (Goods & Services Tax, GST) and Impact on Consumer Expenditure in Townsville / North Queensland, Townsville, Australia.

Fischer, Wolfgang Chr. & Fleming, Ian & Lehnert, Günter (2001) Goods & Services Tax (GST), Consumers' Perceptions after Introduction in Australia in July 2000, Townsville, Australia.

Fischer, Wolfgang Chr. & Massey, Andrew (1994) Consumer Credit in North Queensland, Australia, Department of Economics, Research Monograph, James Cook University, Townsville, Australia.

Fischer, Wolfgang Chr. & Massey, Andrew (1994b) Consumer Affairs in Remote Areas, in: Issues Affecting Rural Communities, Editors: McSwan, D. & McShane, M., Proceedings of the Conference held by The Rural Education Research and Development Centre, at Townsville 10-15 July 1994, James Cook University, Townsville, Australia.

Fleming, Ian (2002) Small Business, in: Wolfgang Chr. Fischer (Editor) Consumers' attitudes towards Weekend, Night & Street Markets, Eul Verlag, Köln, Germany.

Fortin, Bernard & Lacroix, Guy & Montmarquette, Claude (1997) Are Underground Workers More Likely to be Underground Consumers?, Département d'économique, Université Laval, Canada.

Fourastié, Jean (1962) Machinisme et Bien-Etre; Niveau de vie et genre de vie en France de 1700 à nos jours, Paris, France.

Fürth, Henriette (1919) Gemeinwirtschaftliche Förderung der Haushaltung und der Lebenskraft, in: Schriften der Gesellschaft für Soziale Reform, Heft 69, Jena, Germany.

Fürth, Henriette (1915) Die Zentralküche als Kriegseinrichtung, in: Archiv für Sozialwissenschaft und Sozialpolitik, 41. Band, 2. Heft, Tübingen, Germany.

Gallagher, Michael M. (2007) Ausbuy – The protection of Australian Manufacturing Companies in a Global Environment, in: Wolfgang. Chr. Fischer & Kenneth M. Mwenda (Editors) Country of Origin – A Law and Economics Approach to the Concept of Made in Australia, Eul Verlag, Köln, Germany.

Gerhardt, Johannes (1929) Rationalisierung in der Konsumwirtschaft, in: Handwörterbuch der Staatswissenschaften, Jena, Germany.

Gericke, Hans-Jürgen (1967) Der Einfluβ einer rationellen Organisation der Konsumtion in hauswirtschaftlichen Bereich auf die effektive Gestaltung der gesellschaftlichen Produktion, Diss. Halle-Wittenberg, German Democratic Republic.

Giedion, Siegfried (1948) Mechanization takes command; a contribution to anonymous history, New York, USA.

Giles, David E. & Caragata, Patrick J. (1999) Taxes, Risk-Aversion, and the Size of the Underground Economy: A Nonparametric Analysis With New Zealand Data, Econometrics Working Paper EWP 9910, Department of Economics, University of Victoria, Victoria, BC, Canada & Wellington, New Zealand.

Goldring, John (1987) Consumer Protection Law in Australia, 3rd edition, Sydney, Australia.

Haffner, Sebastian (2008) Germany Jekyll and Hyde, An eyewitness analysis of Nazi Germany, with an introduction by Neal Ascherson, Abacus, London, Great Britain.

Hardy, Frank (1983) The Obsession of Oscar Oswald, Carlton, Victoria, Australia.

Hawke, Bob (1986) Prime Minister Launches 'Australian Made' Campaign, Canberra, Australia.

Heinesen, Eskil (1999) The Tax wedge and household demand for services, Economic Modelling, Vol. 16.

Heiskanen, Eva & Pantzar, Mika (1997) Toward Sustainable Consumption: Two New Perspectives, in: Journal of Consumer Policy, Volume 20, No. 4, Dordrecht, Netherland.

Hitchens, Christopher (1999) Goodbye to All That: Why Americans Are Not Taught History, in Harper's Magazine, November, USA.

Homer-Dixon, Thomas F. (2008) The upside of down : the end of the world as we know it and why that may not be such a bad thing, The Text Publishing Company, Melbourne, Australia.

Humphrey, Thomas (1981) Keynes on Inflation, Federal Reserve Bank of Richmond, Economic Review, January/February.

Huxley, Aldous (1958) Brave New World and Brave New World Revisited, HarperCollins, New York, USA.

Jacobeit, Sigrid & Wolfgang (1988) Illustrierte Alltagsgeschichte des deutschen Volkes, 2nd Edition, Vol. 2, Pahl-Rugenstein, Köln, Germany.

Johansen, Anders & Sornette, Didier (2001) 2050: The End of the Growth Era?, Institute of Geophysics and Planetary Physics, University of California at Los Angeles, USA.

Keck, Alfred und Manz, Günter (1967) neue Aspekte der Planung der nichtproduktiven Konsumtion, in: Beiträge zur Lebensstandardforschung,

Schriftenreihe Planung und Leitung der Volkswirtschaft, Berlin, German Democratic Republic.

Keen, Steve (2009) The Roving Cavaliers of Credit, DebtWatch No 31: http://www.debtdeflation.com/blogs/2009/01/31/therovingcavaliersofcredit, January 31st.

Keynes, J. M. (1924) A Tract on Monetary Reform, London.

Kolb, Gerhard (1997) Geschichte der Volkswirtschaftslehre, München, Germany.

Krausbeck, Erich (2002) Isolation of the consumer, in: Wolfgang Chr. Fischer (Editor) Consumers' attitudes towards Weekend, Night & Street Markets, Eul Verlag, Köln, Germany.

König, René (1946) Materialien zur Soziologie der Familie, Beiträge zur Soziologie und Sozialphilosophie, Bd. 1, Bern, Switzerland.

Krelle, Wilhelm (1961) Preistheorie, Tübingen-Zürich, Germany-Switzerland.

Lancaster, Kelvin (1991) Modern Consumer Theory, Brookfield, USA.

Landreth, Harry & Colander, David C. (2002) History of Economic Thought, Houghton Mifflin Company, Boston & Toronto.

Larsen, Gretchen (1998) Rural New Zealand: An Appraisal of Consumer Policy Requirements, Dissertation Master of Commerce Degree, University of Otago, Dunedin, New Zealand.

Lawson, Robert (2001) Email message from England to the author Wolfgang Chr. Fischer.

Lawson, Robert & Tidwell, Paula & Rainbird, Paul & Loudon, David & Della Bitta, Albert (1996) Consumer Behaviour in Australia & New Zealand, McGraw-Hill, Sydney, New York.

Lehnert, Günter (2001) Underground Economy and Tax System: the German Experience, in: Fischer, Wolfgang Chr. & Fleming, Ian & Lehnert, Günter (2001) Goods & Services Tax (GST), Consumers' Perceptions after Introduction in Australia in July 2000, Townsville, Australia.

Lenin, Wladimir Iljitsch (1962) Die groβe Initiative, in: Werke, Bd. 29, Berlin, Germany.

Lenin, Wladimir Iljitsch (1961) Zum internationalen Frauentag (1920), in: Werke, Bd. 30, Berlin, Germany.

Leonard, Richard, SJ (2013) Homily, in: Sacred Heart Cathedral Parish weekly Newsletter 13 January, Townsville, Australia.

Lexis, Wilhelm (1907) Konsumtion, in: Wörterbuch der Volkswirtschaft, 2. Band, zweite, völlig umgearbeitete Auflage, Jena, Germany.

Liefeld, John (2005) Statement to Wolfgang Chr. Fischer on 15-04-2005, Guelph, Canada.

Liefmann, Robert (1922) Die Kommunistischen Gemeinden in Nordamerika, Jena, Germany.

Lloyd, Simon (2005) Consumers across Australia are about to face new, and perhaps unwanted shopping centres as the supermarket war hots up, in: Business Resources Whitepapers (BRW) 14 April, Sydney, Australia.

Lütge, Friedrich (1966) Deutsche Sozial- und Wirtschaftsgeschichte, Ein Überblick, dritte, wesentlich vermehrte und verbesserte Auflage, Berlin-Heidelberg-New York, Germany-USA.

Marsden Jacob Associates (1994) The 'Australian Made' Campaign: Relevance, and General Equilibrium Effects in Unemployment and Full Employment, March, Camberwell, Victoria, Australia.

Marx, Karl & Engels, Friedrich (1848) The Communist Manifesto (Das Kommunistische Manifest), originally titled Manifesto of the Communist Party (German: Manifest der Kommunistischen Partei), Germany.

Maynes, E. Scott (1976) Decision Making for Consumers: An Introduction to Consumer Economics, New York, USA.

McTaggart, Douglas & Findlay, Christopher & Parkin, Michael (1999) Economics, third edition, Melbourne, Australia.

Melbourne Institute of Applied Economic and Social Research, University of Melbourne (2012) Poverty Lines: Australia, June Quarter, Melbourne.

Meyer, Fritz W. (1967) Die Haushaltung in der Nationalökonomie, in: ORDO, Jahrbuch für die Ordnung von Wirtschaft und Gesellschaft, Bd. XVIII, Düsseldorf-München, Germany.

Meyer, Fritz W. (1960) Was bedeutet „Regulation" für die Teilzahlunggsbanken, in: Festschrift zum zehnjährigen Bestehen der Mittelrheinischen Kundenkredit-bank, Dr. Horbach & Co., K. G., Neuwied, Germany.

Meyer-Pollack, Erna (1915) Der Haushalt eines höheren Beamten in den Jahren 1880-1906; untersucht an Hand von Wirtschaftsrechnungen; in: Schriften des Vereins für Sozialpolitik, 145. Bd., München-Leipzig.

Minsky, Marvin (1987) The Society of Mind, New York, p. 26, quoted by Paul Davies (1987).

Morgenstern, Lina (1900) Hilfsbuch zur Gründung, Leitung und Controle von Volksküchen; Kochrezepte der Berliner Volksküchen; Geschichte des Vereins von 1866-1900, 3., erweiterte Aufl., nach 34 jähriger Erfahrung, Berlin, Germany.

Ordinaire, Eduard (1835) Abriβ der von Fourier vorgeschlagenen Einrichtung der lusterweckenden Gewerbsthätigkeit (industrie attrayante), in: Archiv der poltischen Oekonomie und Polizeiwissenschaft, 2. Bd., Heidelberg, Germany.

Ormerod, Paul (1994) Free-Marketeers Opt for Chaos, in Theory, The Age, Melbourne.

Orseu (1995) Measurement of the Shadow Economy, Brussels, Belgium.

Papuc, Andrea (2000) US boom denies euro is money's worth, Black Cash, in: The Australian, Inside Europe, 29-05-00, Sydney, Australia.

Piggott, John & Whalley, John (1998) VAT base broadening, self supply, and the informal sector, Working Paper 6349, National Bureau of Economic Research, Cambridge, MA, USA.

Plassmann, Christa (1969) Die Investitionsleistungen der privaten Haushalte in der BRD; in: Die Finanzen des privaten Haushalts; Festschrift für Walter Kaminsky; Frankfurt.

Queensland Centre for Population Research, University of Queensland Queensland (2008) State and Regional Household and Dwelling Projections 2006 to 2031.

Rees, Martin J. Sir (2003) Our Final Hour – A Scientist's Warning: How Terror, Error, and Environmental Disaster Threaten Humankind's Future in This Century—On Earth and Beyond, Basic Books, New York, USA.

Reichenau, Charlotte von (1943) Die Hauswirtschaft als Produktion und die Wissenschaft, in: Hauswirtschaftliche Jahrbücher, 16. Jg., Heft 2, Stuttgart, Germany.

Reifner, Udo, & Ford, Janet (1992) Banking for People - Social Banking and New Poverty, Consumer Debts and Unemployment in Europe, New York, USA.

Reinert, Erik S. (2013) Civilizing capitalism: "good" and "bad" greed from the enlightenment to Thorstein Veblen (1857-1929), in: real-world economics review, issue no. 63.

Reinert, Erik S. (2012) Neo-classical economics: A trail of economic destruction since the 1970s, in: *real-world economics review*, issue no. 60, 20 June.

Richter, Claire (1919) Das Ökonomiat; Hauswirtschaftlicher Groβbetrieb als Selbstzweck; Berlin, Germany.

Riehl, Wilhelm Heinrich (1965) Die Arbeiter, Eine Volksrede aus dem Jahre 1848, in: Die Eigentumslosen; Der deutsche Pauperismus und die Emanzipationskrise in: Darstellungen und Deutungen der zeitgenössischen Literatur. Hrsg. Carl Jantke und Dietrich Hilger, Freiburg und München, Germany.

Riehl, Wilhelm Heinrich (1930) Die Familie, 3. Auflage, Stuttgart 1861, and: Die Naturgeschichte des Volkes als Grundlage einer deutschen Socialpolitik, Bd. 2: Die bürgerliche Gesellschaft, elfte Auflage, Berlin und Stuttgart, Germany.

Robbins, Lionel (1937) in: Chi-Yuen Wu, An Outline of International Price Theories, George Routledge and Sons.

Rosengren, Peter (2013) Mondragon Co-Operative - The answer to Ford Broadmeadows, The Record, Editor: Archdiocese of Perth, 29 May, Perth, Australia.

Rössler, Hans (1967) Die Konsumtion als Faktor des Wirtschaftswachstums, in: Die Konsumtion im Reproduktionsprozeβ, Beiträge zur sozialistischen

Konsumtionsforschung, Bd. 2, Wissenschaftliche Beiträge der Martin-Luther-Universität Halle-Wittenberg, Halle-Wittenberg, German Democratic Republic.

Rothbard, Murray N. [1995] (2006) Classical Economics: An Austrian Perspective on the History of Economic Thought, Vol. 2, Ludwig von Mises Institute, Auburn, Alabama, USA.

Rothbard, Murray N. [1995] (2006) Economic Thought before Adam Smith: An Austrian Perspective on the History of Economic Thought, Vol. 1, Ludwig von Mises Institute. Auburn, Alabama.

Rothschild, Kurt W. (1992) Economics and Social Problems, Banking for People (Reifner & Ford), New York, USA.

Safe, Mike (2003) War of the Aisles, The Weekend Australian Magazine, 25 Oct, Sydney, Australia.

Saul, John Ralston (2005) The Collapse of Globalism – And the Reinvention of the World, Toronto, Canada.

Schäffle, Albert (1896) Bau und Leben des socialen Körpers, 1. Bd., 2nd edition, 1st & 2nd volume, Tübingen, Germany.

Schmidt, Helmut (2008) Außer Dienst – Eine Bilanz, Siedler Verlag München, Germany.

Schneider, Friedrich & Ernste, Dominik (2000) Schattenwirtschaft und Schwarzarbeit – Umfang, Ursachen, Wirkungen und wirtschaftspolitische Empfehlungen, München-Wien.

Schneider, Friedrich (2001) The Shadow Economy, in: The Economist, No. 3, February.

Schneider, Friedrich (2001) The Size and Development of the Shadow Economies and Shadow Economy Labor Force of 18 Asian and 21 OECD Countries: First Results for the 90s, Paper prepared for the Asia Pacific Finance Association (APFA) Conference 2001 "Rebuilding Our Financial Architecture" to be held in Bangkok, Thailand, July 22-25.

Schweitzer, Rosmarie von (1977) From the economic writings of Aristotle to Home Economics in the German Federal Republic today. In: Journal of Consumer Studies and Home Economics, Stuttgart, Germany.

Seeberg, Stella (1967) Langlebige Haushaltsgüter und Haushaltsinvestitionen, in: Aspekte des hauswirtschaftlichen Strukturwandels, in: Beiträge zue Ökonomie von Haushalt und Verbrauch, Heft 3, Berlin.

Smith, Adrian (1981) A Review of the informal Economy in the European Community, Economic Papers, No. 3, Commission of the European Communities, Directorate-General for Economic and Financial Affairs, Brussels, Belgium.

Smith, Philip M. (1997) Taxes, Deficits, and the Underground Economy, in: The Underground Economy: Global Evidence of its Size and Impact, in: Global

Evidence of its Size and Impact, Section 1, The Fraser Institute Vancouver, BC, Canada.
Sornette, Didier (2009) The Chinese Equity Bubble: Ready to Burst, July 10, 2009; http://arxiv.org/ftp/arxiv/papers/0907/0907.1827.pdf, arXiv, Cornell University, New York, USA.
Southern, David B. (1979) The Revaluation Question in the Weimar Republic, The Journal of Modern History, Vol. 51, No. 1, On Demand Supplement (Mar., 1979), pp. D1029-D1054, Published by: The University of Chicago Press, http://www.jstor.org/stable/1878444
Spiro, Peter S. (1997) Taxes, Deficits, and the Underground Economy, in: The Underground Economy, in: Global Evidence of its Size and Impact, Section 1, The Fraser Institute Vancouver, BC, Canada.
Spiro, Peter S. (1993) Evidence of a Post-GST Increase in the Underground Economy, in: Canadian Tax Journal, Vol. 41, No. 2.
Statistisches Bundesamt (2011) Preise, Fast zehn Jahre Euro – Preisentwicklung vor und nach der Bargeldumstellung, Wiesbaden, Germany.
Statistisches Bundesamt (2010) Wo bleibt mein Geld? Ergebnisse der Einkommens- und Verbrauchsstichprobe 2008, Wiesbaden, Germany.
Statistisches Bundesamt (2009) Zu Hause in Deutschland, Ausstattung und Wohnsituation privater Haushalte, Ausgabe 2009, Wiesbaden, Germany.
Statistisches Bundesamt (2008) Wirtschaftsrechnungen, Einkommens- und Verbrauchs-stichprobe 2008, Ausstattung privater Haushalte mit ausgewählten Gebrauchsgütern, Fachserie 15, Heft 1, Wiesbaden, Germany.
Stavro, Barry (2006) J.K. Galbraith - A critic of his country's materialism, The Sydney Morning Herald, May 1.
Strauβ, Beatrice (1927) Die Konsumtionswirtschaft; Ihre Parallelentwicklung mit der Frauenberufsfrage; Diss. Frankfurt, Germany.
Swan, Peter L. (1987) The Pure Food Laws and Regulations: Burdensome Laws in Search of Meaningful Objectives? Centre for Independent Studies, St. Leonards (NSW), Australia.
Terry, Chris, Ross, Jones & Braddock, Richard (1988) Australian Microeconomic Policies, 3rd edition, New York, Toronto, London.
Tomer, John F. (2012) Brain Physiology, Egoistic and Empathic Motivation, and Brain Plasticity: Toward a More Human Economics, in: World Economic Review, Vol. 1, New York, USA.
Troelstrup, Arch W. (1974) The Consumer in American Society - Personal and Family Finance, fifth edition, New York, USA.
Tschammer-Osten, Berndt (1973) Der private Haushalt in einzelwirtschaftlicher Sicht. Prolegomena zur einzelwirtschaftlichen Dogmengeschichte und Metholodolgie, Berlin, Germany.

Weber, Max (1925) Wirtschaft und Gesellschaft, in: Grundriss der Sozialoekonomik, III. Abteilung, 1. Halbband, zweite, vermehrte Auflage, Tuebingen, Germany.
Wiegand, Bruce & Rothengatter, Maarten (2000) Tax Collection in Australia's Cash Economy: Assessing Revenue Implications, TASA Annual (2000) Conference Proceedings Paper, Flinders University, Adelaide, Australia.
Wikipedia: http://en.wikipedia.org/wiki/Phalanst%C3%A8re, accessed 2 Feb 2012.
Wikipedia: http://en.wikipedia.org/wiki/Soup_kitchen, accessed 27 Feb 2012.
Wikipedia: http://en.wikipedia.org/wiki/Utopian_socialism, accessed 27 Feb 2012.
Wood, Geoffrey E. (1982) Competition, Innovation, Consumer Protection and the Role of the Market in Malcom Fisher, A New Financial Revolution? An international review of the Campbell Report, Centre for Independent Studies, St. Leonards (NSW), Australia.
Wood, Leonie (2004) Meet the stores that say 'love me forever', The Age, 14 April , Melbourne, Australia.
Zenit (2012) The World seen from Rome, The Challenges of Today, 14 December, http://www.zenit.org/english.
Zetkin, Clara (1957) Für die Befreiung der Frau! Rede auf dem internationalen Arbeiterkongress zu Paris, 19. Juli 1889, in: Ausgewählte Reden und Schriften, Bd. 1, Berlin, Germany.
Zetkin, Clara (1926) Lenin ruft die werktätigen Frauen; Artikel Lenins zur Frauenfrage, Berlin, Germany.

Index

-------ℵ------

EINZELSCHRIFTEN

www.ingramcontent.com/pod-product-compliance
Ingram Content Group UK Ltd.
Pitfield, Milton Keynes, MK11 3LW, UK
UKHW020152290926
15471UKWH00005B/832

9 783844 102659